Active labour market policies around the world

Coping with the consequences of globalization

Active labour market policies around the world

Coping with the consequences of globalization

Second edition

Peter Auer, Ümit Efendioğlu and Janine Leschke

International Labour Office   Geneva

ISBN 978-92-2-120456-5

Auer, P.; Efendioğlu, Ü.; Leschke, J:
Active labour market policies around the world:
Coping with the consequences of globalization. Second edition.
Geneva, International Labour Office, 2008

labour policy, employment policy, promotion of employment, developed countries, developing countries
13.01.1

ILO Cataloguing in Publication Data

Photocomposed in Switzerland   BRI
Printed in France   SAD

PREFACE

Active labour market policies (ALMPs) are those policies from the toolkits of policy-makers that combine transfer payments with either work or training activities. They comprise an array of measures from special support for the unemployed, in the form of help with job search, training and education, to subsidies for taking up jobs and job-creation activities such as community work programmes. They are closely interrelated with "passive" labour market policies (e.g. unemployment benefits), as there is today an effort to "activate" the latter in order to enhance the integration of the unemployed and underemployed into the labour market. This book gives an overview of active labour market policies around the world.

Active policies are found in almost all countries of the world but differ in amplitude, design and implementation. Their effectiveness in integrating people into the labour market varies considerably across countries, regions and type of measures. While evaluation research shows that certain measures can indeed enhance the chances for labour market integration, evaluators often find that active programmes are ill adapted to the populations they should serve, suffer from deadweight and substitution effects, and have only a marginal net positive impact. The study finds that this is sometimes due to the type of measures used, but also that traditional evaluation research, which analyses only the employment and earnings effects for participants in programmes, does not include enough factors to evaluate the effects of programmes comprehensively. Additional factors to be considered are, for example, the social cohesion effect or the value of goods and services produced by programme participants.

Beyond these considerations, the study advances some powerful arguments in favour of ALMPs. It shows that the countries most open to the global economy are those that have put in place ALMPs precisely in order to protect their workers from some of the negative employment effects of globalization and technological change. It also demonstrates that workers' perception of security increases with spending on labour market policies, probably because of the protection they enjoy once they lose jobs. Workers' perception of employment/employability security is in turn a factor that influences household consumption and saving behaviour: it can be shown that more secure workers consume more, and that ALMP programmes – beside being an element of macroeconomic spending – also have a stabilizing effect on the economy.

The study concludes with the recommendation that ALMPs should shed their ad hoc nature as a quick-fix crisis solution and become a permanent but adaptable instrument to cope with changes linked to globalization. In such a way they would become an important instrument for labour market intermediation and for more effective labour market governance. The study also recommends new ways of financing and asks for donor cooperation and coordination to provide more funds for ALMPs. It sees social dialogue between governments, employers and workers as one important policy tool to establish a more permanent framework of labour market security, preserving both labour market flexibility and the security which underpins decent work in globalizing economies.

Peter Auer   *Duncan Campbell*
Chief   *Director*
Employment Analysis   *Employment Strategy Department*
and Research Unit

CONTENTS

ACKNOWLEDGEMENTS

The authors are grateful to Janine Berg, Duncan Campbell and Gianni Rosas of the ILO and Günther Schmid of the Wissenschaftszentrum Berlin for their comments. Our thanks go also to Geneviève Domon and Anne Drougard for their patience in integrating many changes into the paper, to Rosemary Beattie, May Hofman and Peter Tallon for editorial work on the first edition, and to Charlotte Beauchamp for editorial work on the second edition.

ABOUT THE AUTHORS

Peter Auer is chief of the Employment Analysis and Research Unit in the Employment Strategy Department of the ILO, Geneva.

Ümit Efendioğlu was formerly research economist at the Employment Analysis and Research Unit and is now with the Cabinet of the Director-General, ILO, Geneva.

Janine Leschke is senior research fellow of the European Trade Union Institute for Research, Education, and Health and Safety, Brussels.

INTRODUCTION

1

It is common to argue that the process of globalization will pressure politicians to make labour markets more flexible … I argue that the opposite may happen. Labour market institutions can be thought of as instruments of social insurance that protect workers against risks for which private insurance is hard to come by. Due to the increased external risks that accompany globalization, the demand for social insurance through a rigid labour market may increase in the future. (Agell, 1999, p. 143)

It is fair to consider both "passive" and "active" labour market policies as one element of such an insurance against the increased risks that labour markets face because of globalization. However, while Agell is right in pointing out the increased risks in labour markets in an era of globalization and the need to cope with these risks through more and/or better social insurance, he is wrong in considering such insurance as being generally part of rigidity. As we will show in more detail below, the elements of social insurance that we analyse here, labour market policies in general and active labour market policies in particular, can also be seen as security devices in flexible labour markets permitting workforce adjustment in a socially acceptable way. Therefore, they potentially allow, rather than hinder, the operation of both the private and the public sectors in an institutional environment that permits flexibility and security. Thus they have a potentially positive economic effect in addition to a positive macroeconomic effect and can be legitimized on economic grounds as well.

However, there is today some controversy on how effective this insurance is, especially when it comes to active labour market policies (ALMPs). Indeed, many evaluation studies have shown a rather marginal labour market improvement for those participating in active programmes. Two citations from recent work on the subject highlight this:

At first sight the bottom line from recent OECD research on the effectiveness of active labour market policies is not terribly encouraging. The track record of many active measures is mixed in terms of raising the future employment and earning prospects of job seekers and producing benefits to society.

... while we cannot ignore the undoubted problems with active measures, it would be wrong to draw a pessimistic conclusion about their potential role in the fight against high and persistent unemployment and the problems of low pay and poverty ... more effective active policies are only one element in a comprehensive strategy of macroeconomic and microeconomic measures required to cut unemployment significantly. Nonetheless, they remain a potentially important weapon in the fight against unemployment. (Martin, 2000, pp. 106-107)

The updated evaluation evidence on active labor market programs largely reinforces the conclusion drawn from earlier reviews. Some ALMPs do have positive impact, with favorable cost-benefit ratios. However, in many cases, programs have not improved the future employment prospects of participants and, when they have, they have not always done so in a cost effective manner ... Despite the mixed evaluation picture, governments, faced with the economic and social problems associated with large numbers of unemployed and poor workers, have little choice but to use active programming as one instrument in their response. (Betcherman, Olivas and Dar, 2004, pp. 51 and 55)

These lengthy quotes from authoritative sources highlight the problems that policy-makers encounter not only in the countries of the Organisation of Economic Co-operation and Development (OECD), but worldwide, when dealing with active labour market policies. **ALMPs are a potentially important weapon in the fight against unemployment and poverty, but produce mixed results**. Compared to regular jobs they are second-best solutions, their objective being to create or enhance access to such regular jobs; but in the absence of enough of the latter, or where the match between the jobs available and those seeking work is poor, there is no way around them.

Two straightforward alternative policy conclusions stem from the above. One is that in the absence of convincing arguments for their effectiveness in practice, active policies should either no longer be used or be drawn upon in small doses only. A second is that the policies should be made more effective for reaching their goals. Having reviewed the available evidence on ALMPs around the world and postulating that we will require more rather than fewer of them to insure against the risks of globalization to employment, this study embraces the latter conclusion, but with some caveats that apply to developing countries, which face problems different from, and more severe than, those confronting most OECD countries. One particular condition for effectiveness is never or extremely rarely met: a fairly balanced quantity – not to speak of quality – of labour supply and demand. "If an economy is generating few vacancies, one should not be surprised if active measures prove to be relatively ineffective" (Martin, 2000, p. 107). This is exactly the case in the majority of developing countries, at least for formal jobs.

The major question, therefore, is whether it makes sense to use active measures to absorb a substantially greater labour supply in the absence of adequate labour demand by the public and private sectors. Would it not be wiser to hold back labour market policy action until effective macroeconomic and microeconomic policies have created sufficient demand to absorb the supply? Is it only qualitative (occupational, qualificational, geographical) matching that makes sense?

While there is indeed a need to have effective employment-creating policies at the macro level, economic and social policies are so interwoven that a well-established active labour market policy – a micro-level policy – is in fact also one, but only one, element of a macroeconomic policy. An employment-oriented macroeconomic policy, which has to be expansionary at least in those spending items that concern employment creation, will necessarily deal with active employment measures such as public works (or in broader terms, employment-intensive infrastructure creation) and enterprise-creation schemes. It will also necessarily make expenditures on labour market related education and training measures.

Therefore, ALMPs (seen as spending items in state budgets or as recipients of donor money) are in fact microeconomic planks of an employment-oriented macroeconomic policy. In addition, there is a consumption smoothing effect of the income replacement part (wages paid) of active schemes that again provides macroeconomic legitimacy to ALMPs. Quiggin (2001) argues that ALMPs could indeed be used as an "automatic stabilizer" in the economy. Spending on programmes would then be anti-cyclical, high when the economy is in recession and unemployment rising, and low when the economy is in a boom and unemployment low.

Macroeconomic legitimacy for ALMPs is one factor, but there is also a value-driven argument that puts some worth on the intrinsic qualities of work as opposed to non-work, especially with regard to transfer benefits. It now seems widely accepted that it is in fact better to finance employment rather than unemployment and to give preference – after an initial period of unemployment benefits with no work, but conditional on job search – to benefits linked to work and training. Therefore, wage replacement benefits for active policies tend to become in-work (or in-training) benefits.

Furthermore, there is a problem with evaluation itself. Two questions are usually included in most evaluations: have participants been inserted into the labour market and have their earnings increased after participation? These two questions, while relevant, are also too narrow, as can be shown by the example of labour-intensive public work schemes. They are usually seen as rather ineffective in achieving labour market reintegration and increasing future wage prospects of participants, partly because they are used as measures of last resort for those hard to place in regular work. However, for a thorough evaluation one needs to include other socio-economic evaluation criteria such as the demand-stimulating effect, the additional wealth effect created through the goods and services produced (e.g. infrastructure) and the social cohesion effect of such schemes. This is particularly true for developing countries, where any question of opportunity costs is usually void: there are not many alternatives to such schemes. And while it holds true that regular, well-paid jobs are preferable, in their absence, the fact of being employed or trained in an active scheme is preferable to poverty, joblessness or underemployment. Notwithstanding the need for social protection without work conditionalities for many categories of people (old-age pensioners, lone mothers with heavy care obligations, certain categories of unemployable disabled persons, etc.), it seems preferable to provide even temporary jobs, socially useful activities or training activities to those able and willing to work.

However, the broader argument in favour of ALMPs in particular, and labour market policies (LMPs) in general, is the need for more insurance against the employment risks linked to globalization.

A rather simple plot of the degree of openness to trade and spending on ALMPs illustrates this point well (figure 1). It suggests that the more open countries are, the better is their insurance against labour market risks, at least in spending terms. Another plot (not shown here) shows that this relationship also exists for total LMP spending. This means that ALMPs are already an important policy instrument for dealing with the consequences of globalization, and more so in the most open countries.

That LMPs can lead to a virtuous cycle of "protected flexibility", allowing firms to adapt to changes caused by globalization and other factors but provides security for workers, is also the conclusion of recent ILO research, which found a positive relationship between workers' perception of employment/employability security and labour market policy spending (Auer, 2003). Figure 2 shows this positive relationship. While this analysis has to be deepened, the conclusions of this study confirm the important place of ALMPs for workers' security in times of change,[1] and the operating of ALMPs as a security device on labour markets has been recently confirmed by the OECD (OECD, 2004).

In order to compensate for the negative employment effects of globalization, such as job losses and a more volatile labour market, a well-developed net of labour market institutions, among which ALMPs figure prominently, seems necessary. ALMPs should therefore also be a major plank of the social dimension of globalization (WCSDG, 2004).

These general legitimating arguments in favour of ALMPs should not detract from the need to improve them constantly and to propose those schemes that work reasonably well. This should indeed strengthen the arguments for the economic and social rationale – beyond the mandate of the ILO – of such schemes.

THE ILO'S MANDATE FOR ACTIVE POLICIES

The Declaration of Philadelphia (1944) recognizes the solemn obligation of the ILO to "further among the nations of the world programmes which will achieve … full employment and the raising of standards of living" and reiterates that the preamble to the Constitution of the ILO provides for the prevention of unemployment and the provision of an adequate living wage. The Universal Declaration of Human Rights of 1948 states that "everyone has the

Figure 1. Spending on ALMPs increases with economic openness

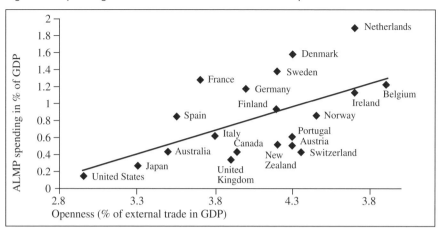

Notes: Ranking established on the basis of the log of the share of total external trade in GDP (average 1970-1990). (Source: Dar and Arnirkhalkhali, 2003.)
Source: ALMP expenditure for 2001: *OECD Employment Outlook 2004.*

Figure 2. Spending on ALMPs increases labour market security

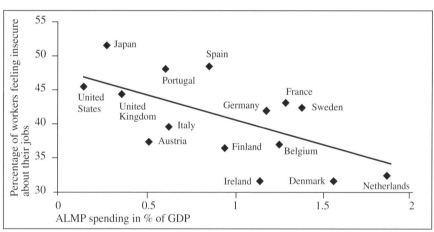

Notes: Job insecurity is the average percentage among worried and unsure people as a percentage of employed. Worried = percentage of workers worried about the future of their company. Unsure = percentage unsure of a job with their company even if they perform well. Using the economic security index of a recent ILO study produces similar results (ILO, 2004).
Source: Data supplied by International Survey research, cited in OECD, 2001a, values for 2000.

right to work, to free choice of employment, to just and favourable conditions of work and to protection against unemployment". It is in the context of these declarations that in 1964 the International Labour Conference adopted the Employment Policy Convention (No. 122) that foresees in Article 1:

> With a view to stimulating economic growth and development, raising levels of living, meeting manpower requirements and overcoming unemployment and underemployment, each Member shall declare and pursue, as a major goal, an **active policy designed to promote full, productive and freely chosen employment**.

ALMPs have to be seen against this background. Although they are only one of the policy areas "to promote full, productive and freely chosen employment", they are an increasingly important element, as witnessed by recent developments towards "activation" of LMPs.

ALMPs are among the ten core elements of the Global Employment Agenda (GEA), adopted by the Committee on Employment and Social Policy of the ILO's Governing Body in March 2003, as one of the most recent attempts at a programme that could stimulate and help ILO member States attain the goals put forward by ILO Declarations and Conventions. ALMPs are also part and parcel of the more general ILO Decent Work Agenda, adopted in 1999, and are a natural element of the fight against poverty, as voiced in the Director-General's 2003 report *Working out of poverty* (ILO, 2003c). Finally, the report of the World Commission on the Social Dimension of Globalization, *A fair globalization: Creating opportunities for all* (WCSDG, 2004), sets the stage for renewed efforts on the part of the ILO to contribute to all policy initiatives and to grasp the opportunities of globalization, while coping with the challenges that occur in labour markets.

This study aims to provide an overview of ALMPs with regard to their extent and effectiveness in the world. This is no easy task, as not only programmes but also information on programmes are unequally distributed around the globe, and observers and analysts can never be sure whether they are faced with the absence of programmes or the absence of information on programmes.

The material analysed in this study tends to indicate that ALMPs are widely used around the world, but that their effectiveness, especially in developing countries, is difficult to gauge. However, lessons learned to date from experience with ALMPs in various countries allow at least an attempt to design a typology and to derive some policy guidelines common to countries with similar characteristics broadly distinguished by regions (developed, transition and developing countries), with a cautionary note against oversimplifying the picture, given the high level of programme diversity both between and within regions.

A brief overview of the historical evolution of ALMPs is provided in Chapter 2, followed by a description of their definition and functions in Chapter 3. Chapter 4 discusses the contribution of ALMPs to the four objectives of employment creation, security in change, equity and poverty reduction. Chapter 5 gives a detailed account of differences in the use of ALMPs in various parts of the world. Chapter 6 examines the ways in which ALMPs can be financed. In Chapter 7, the evaluation of ALMPs in the literature is surveyed in order to assess critically what is known about the effectiveness of these policies. Chapter 8 describes recent trends in ALMPs. The concluding Chapter 9 presents some policy recommendations on the role of ALMPs in the management of change.

Note

[1] Not all LMPs put in place by governments are a consequence of exposure to globalization. There are many other reasons for unemployment and job displacement such as technological change, population growth, and so on.

THE HISTORICAL BACKGROUND OF ALMPS

2

It is probably impossible to put a precise date on the first programme that could be termed an "active labour market policy". However, as an effort by public authorities to provide work when jobs are lacking in the regular labour market, ALMPs were conceptualized and implemented on a fairly large scale during the Great Depression in the 1930s. Initially they were closely associated with quite successful large public works schemes such as those of the New Deal in the United States. Similar programmes also existed in Europe, for example in the inter-war years in Germany. The German experience with such schemes, initiated by the conservative governments during the Weimar Republic, but expanded and transformed into more compulsory schemes by the Nazi government, gave some aspects of ALMPs a lasting negative image.

In their modern form, as instruments for enhancing structural change by ensuring a better (re)-allocation of jobs from low-productivity to high-productivity sectors, ALMPs gained new prominence in the late 1950s, most notably in Sweden, as part and parcel of the Swedish model of economic and societal change. They grew to be more integrated as an instrument of economic and social policy, and their focus shifted to the supply side by using measures to enhance occupational and geographical mobility. However, during cyclical downturns, relief work (community public works schemes) was also used on a massive scale, helping to maintain Sweden in full employment throughout most of the post-war years up to around the 1990s, when proponents of more liberal ideas pressed for less government. Germany acquired a fully fledged arsenal of ALMPs around the 1970s, and France followed suit after the first oil shock. The United States had also developed, in the 1970s, an array of new, mainly supply-side programmes, targeted at vulnerable groups (e.g. the Comprehensive Employment and Training Act (CETA), which provided block grants to states for training and employment programmes) that were subsequently reduced and decentralized in response to complaints of "big government".

With the development of the European Community and later the European Union (EU), ALMPs became important policies to accompany structural change. In the antecedents of the EU, during the time of the European Coal and Steel Community, LMPs – very often early retirement measures but also active policies such as training – were already heavily used to cope with negative employment consequences in the restructured sectors. By 1970, around US$150 million had been spent to provide for around 400,000 laid-off steel and coal workers.

The steady rise of European unemployment rates as a consequence of the oil shocks, as well as various studies indicating that the receipt of long periods of unemployment benefit alone did not result in better access to employment, gradually brought ALMPs back on to the European agenda. The European Employment Strategy (EES) of the European Commission of 1997 made active policies an important policy tool. Policies of activation in particular (the preference of active over passive, income-replacement measures) have once again become an important lever of policy action for employment. The recent focus of EU labour market policies on the topic of protected mobility or "flexicurity" gives an especial new importance to ALMPs as a tool for providing labour market security in globalized economies. [1]

While ALMPs in their modern form were non-existent in the planned economies of the former Eastern bloc, they have been used on a massive scale during the transition to market economies since the 1990s. In some instances, notably in Germany during reunification, one can speak of a transformation through LMPs, as such policies, both active and passive, shouldered a large part of the burden of workforce adjustment. In most other transition countries, both passive and active LMPs were also introduced during the 1990s, and have been extensively used for cushioning labour force adjustment. In developing countries, the history of ALMPs has yet to be written. They have been part of development strategies for quite some time, for example in the form of the public works or training programmes that exist in many countries. ALMPs have gained new ground during the transition from strongly state-run to more market-oriented economic regimes. In China, which has seen tremendous changes in its labour market, the government is about to determine a new framework for making ALMPs (and LMPs in general) a permanent feature of labour market governance.

This brief historical account shows that ALMPs have always had two main and overlapping economic and social functions. One was a temporary bridging of labour demand deficiencies that provided income through work, while the other was a more permanent effort to support the reallocation of labour to alleviate geographical and/or occupational and skill mismatches, while also offering income replacement to those affected. However, neither active nor passive measures were originally conceived to cope with longer-term mass unemployment or chronic underemployment.

Note

[1] According to the recent communication of the EU on flexicurity, besides ALMPs, the three other elements are: labour contracts ensuring stable employment relationships but also adjustment when needed; lifelong learning programmes and initiatives; and modern social security systems, including policies for better integrating work and family responsibilities. On the procedural side, the social dialogue is seen as the main instrument for negotiating flexicurity solutions (EU Commission, 2007).

DEFINITION AND FUNCTIONS
OF LMPS AND ALMPS

3

Labour market policies (LMPs) are defined here as policies that provide income replacement and labour market integration measures to those seeking work, usually the unemployed, but also the underemployed and the employed who are looking for better jobs. So-called "passive" policies are concerned with providing replacement income during periods of joblessness or job search, while "active" policies refer to labour market integration through demand- or supply-side measures.[1] Hence the main thrust of ALMPs is active support for labour market integration. Passive policies, on the other hand, correspond to social transfers that are not conditional upon joining a training or work programme, though they usually include job search provisions that are increasingly enforced and correspond to an active element in passive policies. Active policies, in contrast, are explicitly contingent upon participation in programmes that enhance labour market (re)integration.

Typical passive programmes are unemployment insurance, unemployment assistance and early retirement. Typical active measures, on the other hand, are labour market training, job creation in the form of public and community work programmes, enterprise creation programmes and employment subsidies. Active policies are usually targeted at specific groups facing particular labour market integration difficulties, such as younger and older people, women and those particularly hard to place, such as the disabled. In part, ALMPs are also an answer to the growing criticism that pure income replacement policies might entail disincentives to work once unemployment becomes of longer duration.

Active as well as passive LMPs intermediate between supply and demand on the labour market. Indeed, the primary economic function assigned to LMPs is the matching of labour demand and supply. The impact of LMP intervention on labour supply and demand can vary. Such policies contribute either directly to matching (e.g. public and private employment services, job search assistance, prospecting and registering vacancies, profiling, providing labour market information), or to enhancing supply (e.g. training and retraining), reducing supply (e.g. early retirement), creating demand (e.g. public works, enterprise creation and self-employment) or changing the structure of demand (e.g. employment subsidies), for example in favour of disadvantaged groups.

There are also specific and important sub-functions of LMPs, such as the provision of replacement income during sometimes lengthy matching periods (the time between an unemployment spell and being hired for a job) and thus the alleviation of poverty linked to joblessness, the maintenance and enhancement of employability, the establishment or upkeep of infrastructure, the creation of businesses, and others. All of these are intended to have positive effects on social integration.

It has often been argued that ALMPs are second-best solutions, of value only in the absence of regular jobs. This proposition should be qualified: the idea that one day the need for ALMPs will have vanished, because there will be sufficient regular jobs, seems false. It may hold true for public works schemes and other demand-oriented measures, but there will always be a need for the supply-side elements such as labour market training, enhanced job search and all measures that provide employability. This applies also to public and private employment services. It is hard to imagine a labour market that can live without intermediary institutions, of which ALMPs are a significant component.

There should be a constant effort to render these institutions and policies efficient. The fact that flows of people transiting through the intermediary institutions swell and shrink because of the structural and cyclical changes in an economy poses a challenge to management of the intermediary structure. However, while the institutions must be flexible to respond to this, the principle of a permanent need for these intermediary structures must be asserted.

LABOUR MARKET INTERMEDIATION AND ALMPS

Figures 3 and 4 show schematically the main institutions of the matching process in the labour market. While in standard labour economics the supply/demand curve of labour is determined by the price of labour (wages), in the real economy institutions interfere in this process. There is a constant mismatch between supply and demand, and therefore one observes constant flows on labour markets. People lose jobs, labour market entrants and re-entrants look for jobs, and those with jobs also look for better jobs. But new jobs are usually rationed.

Ideally, workers who voluntarily or involuntarily quit the shrinking part of the private or public sector and the new labour market entrants who constitute labour supply should be (re)allocated to the expanding, supposedly more productive parts of the economy, defined by the new labour demand. But there are numerous obstacles before such matching can take place: even if we assume that the quantities of supply and demand are in equal sum, jobs lost and jobs created are usually in different locations, different sectors and different occupations. Workers may have different skills from those in demand, may differ in age and sex, may ask for different wages, and so on. In short, the labour force is not homogeneous and there are mismatches between supply and demand resulting in frictional and – when such differences remain steady – in structural unemployment.

However, in transition and developing countries, and even in many industrialized Western developed countries, we cannot assume that supply and demand are numerically equal or even similar. In most developing and transition countries, supply is indeed much greater than (formal) labour demand.

There is thus a major challenge with regard to labour markets: both quantitative and qualitative mismatches have to be balanced. For many economists who treat the labour force as fairly homogenous, flexible wages and some training would provide the miracle cure and lead to labour market clearing. Unrealistic as this is for developed countries, it is even a more misleading conception for developing countries: wage "dumping", leading to low effective demand in regions that suffer from chronic over-supply of labour, is indeed one of the causes of underdevelopment.

In such situations, a much better road is through building institutions that should be seen as bridges between supply and demand. This is what we call "labour market intermediation", comprising the whole array of labour market institutions, with labour market policies at the core. Labour market intermediation consists of policies and institutions such as passive and active LMPs and their delivery institutions (both public and private employment services, training institutions, municipalities, non-governmental organizations (NGOs) and even private companies), whose overarching task is the matching of supply and demand on the labour markets. Labour market information systems are also part of the intermediation structure.

Figures 3 and 4 show the working of such an intermediary structure: it sits in the middle of supply and demand and deals with the part of the supply flow of workers that does not spontaneously (or effectively) meet the demand flow. As this system is in constant movement, figures 3 and 4 also show entry, exit and stable positions within the private and public sectors. They also show the differences between developed and developing countries: apart from the situation of over-supply, the dominance of the informal economy for surplus labour absorption, as well as the fact that we expect significant outflows from the intermediary to the informal economy (for example, after the ending of some employment schemes), are depicted.

One important question here is: does it make sense to have intermediary structures in the absence of sufficient demand for labour? Or, to use the bridge metaphor, is this a bridge leading nowhere? The answer cannot be complete, but some elements are clear: creating only the intermediary structure will not do the job. It also needs to be backed up by adequate policies at other levels, such as efficient macroeconomic and structural policies that attract investment, and create and support labour demand. But one surely cannot wait for the construction of an efficient intermediary (all countries have elements of it, as will be shown below) until there is sufficient formal demand to absorb the huge

Figure 3.   Labour market flows: developed countries

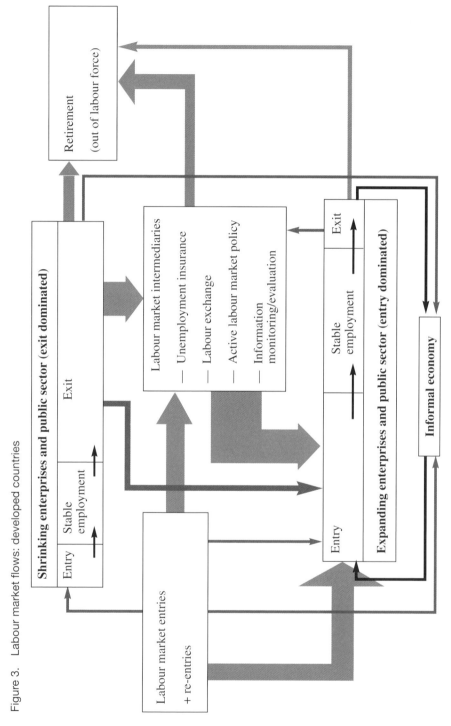

Figure 4. Labour market flows: developing countries

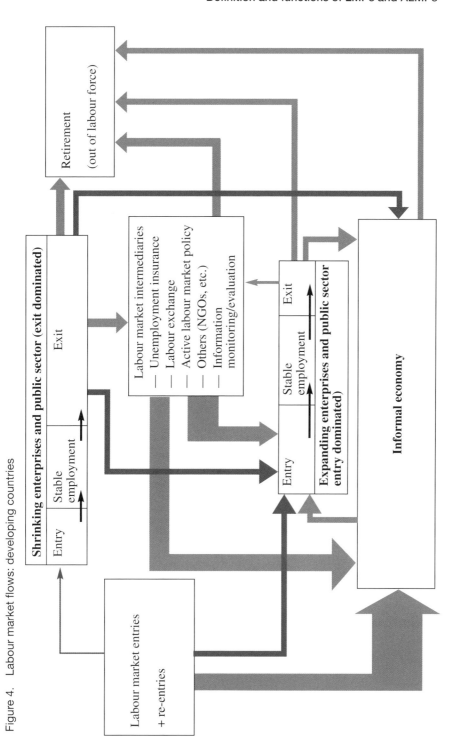

supply flows. While the proposition, originally made for goods markets, that "supply creates its own demand" (J.B. Say), does not hold entirely true for labur markets, there is some value in investing in the skills of the labour force as this could trigger more active job search, increase the available options and lead, for example, to small enterprise creation. However, in the absence of sufficient labour demand, the demand elements of the intermediary structure, such as demand-side ALMPs (for example, public works schemes and enterprise creation schemes), might also be given preference over the pure supply-side schemes such as training, although one could integrate the latter into the former. One has also to see the whole intermediary structure as a management tool supporting flows: indeed, it should be seen as a permanent structure of policies and institutions that provide people with capabilities (Sen, 1989) by offering them temporary participation in such permanent structures, thereby facilitating their insertion into the labour market. From this perspective, one can be assertive: labour market intermediation – based partially on ALMPs – is an indispensable element of labour markets in market economies, and thus a crucial instrument of labour market governance.

Note

[1] In labour market literature and in OECD and EU databases, the terms passive and active LMPs are typically used to distinguish between income support only (passive) and income support plus training or work (active). It might therefore be appropriate to speak of income replacement with (active) and without (passive) work or training conditionalities.

THE CONTRIBUTION OF ALMPS
TO THE OBJECTIVES OF EMPLOYMENT
CREATION, SECURITY IN CHANGE,
EQUITY AND POVERTY REDUCTION

4

ALMPs can have multiple functions, depending on the objectives they are used for. They play an important role in contributing to direct and indirect employment creation in the regular as well as in the informal labour market. Since participation in ALMPs is usually associated with some income transfer, they are also a significant poverty prevention measure. In contrast to passive unemployment compensation, they not only compensate people financially but often also contribute to an improvement in the participants' employability and thus increase their re-employment prospects. ALMPs can also be used to achieve greater equity by favouring more disadvantaged labour market groups. In addition to these functions, they are also one of the imperative measures that help create more income and employability security in times of multiple labour market changes. This chapter briefly reviews these four functions of ALMPs.

ALMPS AND EMPLOYMENT CREATION

ALMPs support employment creation in two basic ways: directly by job-creation measures (e.g. public works and enterprise creation, as well as hiring subsidies); and indirectly by improving employability through training and by ensuring efficient labour exchanges that provide better labour market information and enhanced job matching. There are also indirect positive macro-economic effects through consumption smoothing during economic downturns (see the box on "Consumption smoothing through LMP expenditure" in Chapter 6) and positive spill-over effects of infrastructure creation, for example, through public works schemes.

ALMPS AND SECURITY IN CHANGE

In today's globalized economies, characterized by openness to trade and investment, continuous technological progress and privatization of state-owned enterprises, labour market changes are inevitable. In many cases, these changes result not only in internal reallocation of labour but also in massive lay-offs. As a consequence, governments must find ways to cope with such changes. In this respect, ALMPs are an important policy tool for addressing the adverse effects of structural change and insufficient labour demand, thus creating security in change. But they also have to be complemented by macroeconomic policies of economic growth and employment creation.[1] In the absence of a favourable macro environment for increased investment, growth and employment, ALMPs can only provide temporary support to the unemployed.

Active policies must contribute to the reallocation of workers made redundant, while offering them replacement incomes during transition. In such a way, ALMPs contribute not only to security in change but also to employment growth, at least in the longer run. The ILO has already advised constituents on such active ways to cope with redundancies (e.g. socially responsible restructuring, community-based restructuring).[2]

ALMPS AND EQUITY

ALMPs also contribute to equity. One straightforward task is to ensure the participation of specific target groups in programmes that serve disadvantaged persons. ALMPs should seek to promote the advancement of those individuals usually hired last and thus prevent creaming.[3] This implies overcoming discrimination against older workers, the least qualified, ethnic groups and the disabled. It also means eliminating discrimination against women (ILO, 2003b).

ALMPs must also address the labour market insertion challenges facing youth. The Youth Employment Network (YEN), a joint initiative of the United Nations, the World Bank and the ILO, is an important project in this context. Young people should not start their working life with a prolonged period of unemployment. Rather, they should be given access to training or work-based alternatives in the absence of regular jobs. Inserting young people into the labour market is essential for successful management of demographic change and accordingly also contributes to the goal of security in change. It seems that while some fear a trade-off between younger and older workers (an extra effort for the young being assumed to displace older workers), data on the employment rates of older and younger cohorts in industrialized countries show that high employment rates for older workers usually correlate positively with high youth employment rates, thus pointing to complementarities rather than trade-offs.

On a more general level, ALMPs can contribute to equity during waves of structural change and recession by maintaining income at a level that does not result in large increases in wage dispersion. This also applies to unemployment benefits and has a bearing on poverty alleviation.

ALMPS' CONTRIBUTION TO POVERTY REDUCTION

ALMPs contribute to poverty alleviation through measures that provide work, training and income. The idea that decent work is the best insurance against poverty is also at the heart of ALMPs (ILO, 2003c). In the absence of regular jobs, but also as a support to job creation, ALMPs can contribute to poverty alleviation. For example, income derived from active work or training programmes is important for otherwise unemployed individuals, not least because of the socially integrating effect of decent work. For the developed world and the transition countries, it can be demonstrated that transfers related to work and training are often a better alternative, in terms of the opportunity costs of public spending, than unemployment benefits alone. For developing countries, the target group for ALMPs might not be the openly unemployed, but rather the working poor in the informal economy. This requires new insights into the labour market behaviour of the working poor and into how ALMPs can contribute to formalizing and increasing the productivity and security of informal jobs.

There are thus, in principle, ample reasons for using ALMPs to attain the objectives of employment creation, security in change, equity and poverty reduction, and ALMPs have indeed been used for these purposes in all parts of the world. However, their use has varied considerably across countries. In Chapter 5, information is presented on differences in ALMP spending and participation around the world. A variety of examples of ALMP measures in different regions of the world are also discussed, in order to highlight the diversity of programmes and experiences corresponding to countries at different levels of development and to draw some policy lessons.

Notes

[1] Workers' security is also affected by economic growth. All other things being equal, enhanced growth and employment creation lead to an enhanced individual perception of security: security is highest in boom times, and when LMPs and ALMPs exist. See Auer and Cazes (2003).

[2] See, for example, Hansen (2001), Esser et al. (2003), Rogovsky (2005).

[3] A contrary movement can be observed in EU Member States, which have lately pursued preventive policy strategies in order to avoid long-term unemployment. There is a general trend away from ALMPs targeted to long-term unemployment and towards the early inclusion of the unemployed in active policies.

DIFFERENCES IN THE UTILIZATION OF ALMPS: DEVELOPED, TRANSITION AND DEVELOPING COUNTRIES

5

OVERVIEW OF EXPENDITURE ON AND PARTICIPATION IN ALMPS

The policy framework for ALMPs has mainly, but not exclusively, been developed in the industrialized countries, where most evaluation research has also been undertaken. But these programmes have since been locally adapted and applied in other parts of the world. The so-called transition countries, for example, made extensive use of ALMPs during the transformation of their planned economies to market economies. Developing countries are also increasingly implementing ALMPs to mitigate adverse labour market effects of economic crises, as well as to establish some security for workers affected by structural change, as the East Asian experience clearly illustrates.[1] While it is difficult to give an exact picture of the diversity of programmes in the world, mainly due to lack of data for many developing countries, some comparative information on expenditure on both active and passive LMPs, as well as on programme participation, is provided below.

In the **OECD countries**, and especially in the 15 EU Member States (prior to the accession of 10 others in 2004 and two in 2007), ALMPs have become a permanent feature of economic and social policy. Expenditure on LMPs fluctuates anti-cyclically, mostly because spending on passive policies, in particular unemployment benefits, increases during an economic downturn, while spending on ALMPs is usually more stable over the cycle.[2] Thus, for example, at the beginning of the recovery in 1993 around 3.63 per cent of GDP in the EU was spent on LMPs, of which 1.13 per cent (approximately one-third) was spent on ALMPs. In 1998, however, five years into the recovery, overall spending was down to 2.8 per cent of GDP, a reduction of 0.83 percentage points, while spending on ALMPs, corresponding to 1.07 per cent of GDP, had fallen by just 0.06 percentage points (OECD, 2001). Figure 5 indicates that this behaviour might have changed, especially since 2003, which shows stable expenditure on PLMPs around the 1.4 per cent level, but a decline in ALMPs. However, these figures are not comparable with former OECD data and do not include spending on PES.

Figure 5. Expenditure on LMPs and unemployment rates in EU-15 countries, 1999-2005

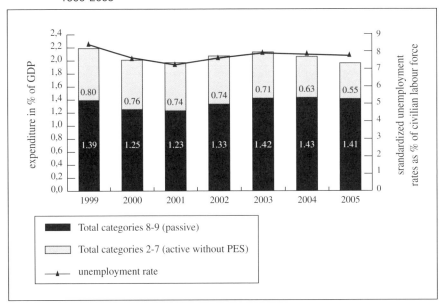

Note: EU averages for expenditure on PES are available only from 2004 onwards. For 2004 and 2005 they lie at 0.23% and 0.24% of GDP, respectively.
Source: Eurostat, 2007, extraction 2007/08/02; OECD (2007a).

ALMP spending in the EU is also attributable to the activation strategy, favouring active over passive spending, as depicted in the EES. Although the EU-15 countries' average spending on ALMPs is markedly above that of all other regions reviewed, there are nevertheless strong differences between individual countries. The Nordic countries and the Netherlands historically spend a substantial amount on ALMPs, while Greece and the United Kingdom are low spenders.

In comparison to the EU-15 countries, among the industrialized countries as a whole the 2005 OECD data indicate relatively low public expenditure on passive as well as on active measures for the United States and Japan (table 1).

The **transition countries** are low spenders on ALMPs . The EU accession countries for which data are available still spend considerably less on LMPs – especially on passive labour market policies and on labour market services – than EU-15 countries on average (table 2). The same is true for Croatia, the Russian Federation and Ukraine (table 3). With a view to accession to the EU, candidate countries progressively adapted national labour legislation, institutions and policies. While there were no important changes in replacement rates between the late 1990s and 2003, there was a slight tendency towards increasing the maximum duration of benefits for specific categories of workers (older workers in the Czech Republic; workers in problematic regions in

Table 1. Public expenditure on LMPs as a percentage of GDP in selected OECD countries, 2005

Country[a]	PES and administration	Training	Job rotation / job sharing	Employment incentives	Supported employment and rehabilitation	Direct job creation	Start-up incentives	Out-of-work income maintenance and support	Early retirement	Total	Total ALMP*	PLMP**
Australia	0.26	0.04	-	0.01	0.05	0.08	0.01	0.61	-	1.06	0.45	0.61
Austria	0.17	0.33	-	0.05	0.04	0.04	0.01	1.23	0.28	2.13	0.62	1.51
Belgium	0.23	0.20	-	0.17	0.12	0.36	-	1.94	0.42	3.45	1.08	2.37
Canada	0.16	0.08	-	0.01	0.02	0.02	0.01	0.62	-	0.95	0.32	0.62
Czech Republic	0.13	0.01	-	0.04	0.04	0.03	-	0.24	-	0.49	0.25	0.24
Denmark	0.31	0.51	-	0.45	0.48	-	-	1.83	0.68	4.26	1.74	2.51
Finland	0.18	0.37	-	0.11	0.10	0.07	0.02	1.47	0.44	2.79	0.89	1.90
France	0.24	0.29	-	0.13	0.07	0.18	-	1.57	0.06	2.52	0.90	1.62
Germany	0.35	0.25	-	0.05	0.13	0.10	0.09	2.30	0.05	3.32	0.97	2.35
Greece	..	0.03	-	0.02	-	-	-	0.35	-	..	..	0.35
Hungary	0.09	0.04	-	0.10	-	0.06	-	0.38	0.01	0.68	0.29	0.39
Ireland	0.12	0.24	-	0.05	0.01	0.21	-	0.77	0.06	1.46	0.63	0.83
Italy	0.08	0.20	-	0.20	-	0.01	0.05	0.72	0.10	1.36	0.54	0.82
Japan	0.19	0.04	-	0.02	-	-	-	0.44	-	0.68	0.25	0.43
Rep. of Korea	0.03	0.04	-	0.02	0.02	-	0.01	0.22	-	0.35	0.13	0.22
Luxembourg	0.06	0.13	0.05	0.19	0.01	0.13	-	0.47	0.20	1.19	0.52	0.67
Mexico	-	0.01	-	-	-	-	0.01	-	-	0.02	0.02	-
Netherlands	0.49	0.13	-	0.02	0.53	0.15	-	2.02	-	3.35	1.33	2.02
New Zealand	0.12	0.17	-	0.02	0.06	-	0.01	0.44	-	0.83	0.39	0.44
Norway	0.12	0.37	-	0.03	0.15	0.07	-	0.87	-	1.62	0.75	0.87
Poland	0.07	0.10	-	0.04	0.16	0.03	0.03	0.31	0.55	1.29	0.43	0.86
Portugal	0.17	0.29	-	0.16	0.04	0.03	-	1.19	0.09	1.98	0.69	1.29
Slovakia	..	0.02	-	0.03	0.01	0.06	0.05	0.17	0.09	..	..	0.27
Spain	0.13	0.17	0.01	0.30	0.02	0.09	0.06	1.42	0.03	2.23	0.78	1.45

Table 1. (Cont.)

Country[a]	PES and administration	Training	Job rotation / job sharing	Employment incentives	Supported employment and rehabilitation	Direct job creation	Start-up incentives	Out-of-work income maintenance and support	Early retirement	Total	Total ALMP*	PLMP**
Sweden	0.23	0.34	0.05	0.45	0.22	-	0.03	1.20	-	2.52	1.32	1.20
Switzerland	0.14	0.29	-	0.08	0.25	-	0.01	0.93	-	1.69	0.76	0.93
United Kingdom	0.38	0.09	-	0.01	0.01	-	-	0.19	-	0.68	0.49	0.19
United States	0.03	0.05	-	-	0.03	0.01	-	0.24	-	0.38	0.13	0.24

-     nil or less than 0.005%.

..   no data available.

a   No data for Iceland and Turkey.

*   ALMP is the sum of the first seven columns.

**   PLMP is the sum of the eighth and ninth columns.

Source: OECD, 2007a; data extracts 2 Aug. 2007.

Poland) (Cazes and Nesporova, 2007, pp. 42-44). Over the same period, there were no coherent trends in expenditure on ALMPs per unemployed person. Spending increased significantly in some countries (such as Bulgaria and the Czech Republic), declined rather sharply in others (Poland and Slovenia) and stagnated in the remainder. Reforms in these areas are continuing: Croatia and Lithuania, for example, recently increased unemployment benefit levels, and both countries, as well as Poland, also increased the duration of benefit payments, especially for the elderly. Similarly, the Hungarian unemployment benefit system has been reformed in 2005; active job search is now a key requirement (for more information see Frey, 2007, pp. 129-39). Bulgaria, on the other hand, in line with the requirements of the EES, has considerably increased its ALMPs in the pre-accession period (Beleva et al., 2007, pp. 76-80). In 2005, among the transition countries that are now EU members ALMP spending was highest in Bulgaria (0.44 per cent) and lowest in Estonia (0.05 per cent). Spending on labour market services is highest in Slovakia and very low in Estonia and Romania (table 2).

In **Latin America**, the unweighted average of public expenditure on ALMPs (training and employment programmes only) in seven countries amounted to 0.4 per cent of GDP in 1997,[3] somewhat above the level in the transition countries. The high spenders among these seven countries were Costa Rica, Jamaica and Mexico, while the low spenders were Argentina, Chile and Peru. However, breaking down expenditure into training and employment programmes reveals that Mexico and Jamaica led the league in terms of spending on employment generation programmes (approximately 0.50 per cent of GDP), whereas Costa Rica spent most on training programmes (0.73 per cent of GDP) (table 4). Among the three countries for which we have 2002 data, Argentina spends most (table 5). In 2000 expenditure on LMPs in Argentina was still only around 0.30 per cent of GDP; the subsequent increase was mainly due to the Programa de Jefes y Jefas de Hogar Desocupados, which was launched in 2002 (Marshall, 2004, pp. 35 ff.).

Active measures were also enacted in most **East Asian countries** after the 1997 Asian financial crisis, but public expenditure on ALMPs in these countries is lower than the OECD average. The Republic of Korea, for instance, reports spending on ALMPs of 0.13 per cent of GDP in 2005 (see table 1).

In **Africa**, active measures are also a commonly used policy tool, according to evidence provided by recent ILO studies.[4] Some countries, such as Algeria and Tunisia, report expenditure on ALMPs at above 1 per cent of GDP, although no data on the amount of overall regional spending exist. In 1995, Egypt and Morocco reported spending on public works of 0.3 per cent of GDP, Yemen 0.2 per cent, Tunisia 0.4 per cent and Algeria 0.6 per cent (see Handoussa and Tzannatos, 2002, p. 144).

It appears that ALMPs are used in all parts of the world, although their role is sometimes only marginal. The EU (especially the EU-15 countries) is clearly taking the leading role, mainly because of a deliberate policy that

Table 2. Expenditure on LMP as percentage of GDP in selected EU transition countries, 2005

	Labour market services	Training	Job rotation/ job sharing	Employment incentives	Integration of the disabled	Direct job creation	Start-up incentives	Out-of-work income maintenance and support	Early retirement	Total LMP	ALMP*	PLMP
EU-15	0.24[a]	0.21[a]	0.003[a]	0.13[a]	0.09[a]	0.08[a]	0.03[a]	1.33[a]	0.08[a]	2.20[a]	0.55[a]	1.41[a]
Bulgaria	0.07	0.07	-	0.04	0.01	0.32	0.01	0.22	-	0.73	0.44	0.22
Czech Republic	0.13	0.01	-	0.04	0.04	0.03	0.00	0.24	-	0.49	0.12	0.24
Estonia	0.02	0.03	-	0.01	-	-	0.01	0.12	-	0.19	0.05	0.12
Latvia	0.06	0.10	-	0.02	0.01	0.03	-	0.32	-	0.54	0.15	0.32
Lithuania	0.07	0.05	-	0.04	0.00	0.05	0.00	0.11	0.02	0.34	0.15	0.12
Hungary	0.09[a]	0.04	-	0.10	-	0.06	0.00	0.38	0.01	0.68[a]	0.20	0.39
Poland	:	0.10	n	0.04	0.16	0.03	0.03	0.31	0.55	:	0.36	0.86
Romania	0.03	0.01	-	0.05	-	0.04	0.00	0.36	-	0.49	0.10	0.36
Slovakia	0.17	0.02	-	0.03	0.01	0.06	0.05	0.17	0.10	0.61	0.17	0.27

-    not applicable.
n   not significant.
:   data not available.
*   Excludes labour market services.
a   Estimated values.

Source: Eurostat, 2007; data extracted 9 Aug. 2007.

Table 3. Expenditure on LMP in selected transition countries, 1998 (percentage of total expenditure on LMPs plus the cost of running the National Employment Service (NES), if not otherwise stated)

Country	Active LMP	Of which in			Passive LMP	Costs of NES	Total expenditure, US$ million	Total expenditure, % of GDP	Expenditure on ALMPs (active LMP + NES) as % of GDP
		LMT	PW	SE					
Croatia	4.2		n.a.		80.0	15.8	112.66	0.6	0.12
Russian Fed.	11.2	7.8[a]		3.4	65.8	23.0	921.01	0.2	0.07
Ukraine	10.3	8.7	1.0	0.6	63.7	26.0	0.30	0.3	0.11

LMT = labour market training;
PW = public works;
SE = subsidized employment and other programmes;
NES = National Employment Service.
a   Combined expenditure on labour market training and public works programmes.

Source: O'Leary et al. (2001), p. 43.

Table 4. Expenditure on training and employment generation programmes
in seven countries in Latin America and the Caribbean, c.1997

Country	Expenditure on: Training programmes		Employment generation	
	US$000s	As % of GDP	US$000s	As % of GDP
Argentina	95.6	0.04	249.2	0.09
Brazil	310.2	0.10	1 188.8	0.21
Chile	18.3	0.03	1.4	0.00
Costa Rica	60.6	0.73	3.3	0.04
Jamaica	18.6	0.44	21.2	0.50
Mexico	135.0	0.04	1 802.0	0.51
Peru	5.0	0.10	0.1	0.00

Source: Márquez (1999), p. 11.

Table 5. Expenditure on LMP as percentage of GDP
in selected Latin American countries, 2001/2002

Expenditure	Argentina (2002)*	Brazil (2001)	Mexico (2001)
Total	0.99	0.59[a]	(0.13)[b]
Employment programmes	0.80	0.08[a]	(0.13)[b]
Unemployment insurance	0.19	0.43[a]	-

*   Preliminary data.

-     not applicable.

[a]   Fund for Worker Protection (unemployment insurance or *abono salarial*: a wage supplement of one minimum wage to be paid to all workers employed in the formal sector who earn up to twice the minimum wage), training schemes, intermediation and support to micro-enterprises and small firms.

[b]   Programa de Empleo Temporal, support for low-income producers, and fund for assisting micro-enterprises and small and medium firms.

Source: Marshall (2004), pp. 28, 37.

promotes employment – and specifically active policies – as an important part of its EES.

Programme participation rates also reveal considerable differences between countries.[5] In industrialized OECD countries participation rates above 4 per cent of the labour force emerge in Belgium, Denmark, Germany, Sweden and the Netherlands, while participation in Australia and New Zealand is comparatively low (table 6); however, it should be noted that many countries do not report participation rates. Among EU transition countries (table 7), Slovakia and Bulgaria take the lead; for all other countries that provide data, participant stocks are lower than among EU-15 countries, and are especially low in Estonia. Among non-EU transition countries, the Russian Federation displayed relatively high ALMP participation rates (measured as a proportion of the average monthly number of registered jobseekers) in the late 1990s (table 8). Of the Latin American countries in the late 1990s, Argentina showed comparatively high participation rates measured as a percentage of the labour force, while Peru took the last place among the countries compared (table 9). However, international comparisons are difficult because of a lack of data for certain regions, as well as a lack of comparable data.

Comparisons of raw input (spending) and raw output (participation) variables are meaningless in the absence of corrections, for example, for programme duration (some countries serve large numbers for a short time, while others serve smaller numbers over a longer term) or programme quality (wage levels paid to participants, equipment, training locality, type of public works programme, additional help, for example in the form of work and family reconciliation measures, etc.). Therefore, they can only be a departure point for a more thorough analysis of the cost-effectiveness of active measures. Comparative work on Europe shows, for example, that if Dutch and Danish ratios are controlled for by programme duration, 1 per cent of GDP spending on ALMPs would result in 2.9 per cent of labour force participation in Denmark and 0.9 per cent in the Netherlands.[6] This confirms that the Netherlands would need to spend more than 3 per cent of its GDP to arrive at the same participation rates as Denmark. This analysis does not, however, control for the quality of the programmes.

Most importantly, raw input and output indicators are not always good predictors of outcomes. If, for example, the amount a country spends on 1 per cent of its unemployed is controlled for, thus broadly controlling for the population eligible for labour market measures, the following picture emerges. Compared to other Western and Eastern European countries, Denmark spends by far the most on its unemployed (see figures 6 and 7). However, only more sophisticated evaluation would reveal anything about the outcomes for the participants, i.e. whether integration into the labour market was successful, whether employment is sustainable or decent, whether a return to unemployment is likely, and so on (see Chapter 7 on evaluation).

Table 6. Participant stocks in LMPs as percentage of the labour force in selected OECD countries, 2005 [a]

Country [a]	PES and administration	Training	Job rotation / job sharing	Employment incentives	Supported employment and rehabilitation	Direct job creation	Start-up incentives	Out-of-work income maintenance and support	Early retirement	Total	Total ALMP* (excl.PES and admin)	PLMP**
Australia	..	0.28	-	-	0.75	0.69	0.05	5.51	-	..	1.77 [a]	5.51
Austria	..	1.89	-	1.11	..	0.14	0.06	5.67	1.57	..	..	7.24
Belgium	..	2.74	-	1.47	0.65	2.06	0.02	13.26	2.33	..	6.95	15.59
Canada	..	1.58	-	0.15	..	0.06	0.12	..	-	..	2.45	..
Czech Republic	..	0.12	-	0.45	0.31	0.18	0.11	2.68	-	..	1.16	2.68
Denmark	..	1.79	-	1.27	2.14	-	-	7.00	2.76	..	5.20	9.76
Finland	..	1.86	0.26	0.74	0.32	0.37	0.14	9.70	1.82	..	3.69	11.52
France	..	1.98	-	..	0.46	0.96	0.24	9.32	0.38	..	3.64	9.70
Germany	..	2.35	0.01	0.26	0.39	0.89	0.83	16.47	0.22	..	4.73	16.68
Hungary	..	0.34	-	..	-	0.39	0.10	3.08	0.13	..	..	3.21
Ireland	..	..	-	0.31	0.09	1.21	0.26	7.29	0.55	..	..	7.84
Italy	..	..	0.07	2.71	-	0.18	..	2.83	0.39	..	..	3.22
Luxembourg	..	1.22	-	..	-	0.96	..	3.57	0.65	..	..	4.22
Netherlands	..	1.31	-	0.29	2.08	0.49	-	9.22	-	..	4.17	9.22
New Zealand	..	0.57	-	..	1.35	..	..	2.44	-	..	1.91	2.44
Norway	..	1.64	-	0.23	0.47	0.33	0.02	4.36	-	..	2.68	4.36
Poland	..	0.65	-	..	..	0.06	0.02	2.18	2.92	..	..	5.10
Portugal	..	0.92	-	..	..	0.38	0.11	5.46	0.22	..	..	5.68
Slovakia	..	0.17	-	0.59	0.27	4.02	0.43	1.46	0.62	..	5.47	2.07
Spain	..	1.41	0.41	..	0.20	..	..	6.20	-	..	..	..
Sweden	..	1.07	0.21	2.25	0.74	-	0.12	7.64	-	..	4.39	7.64
Switzerland	..	0.91	-	0.68	0.87	-	0.02	3.62	-	..	2.48	3.62
United Kingdom	..	0.74	-	..	..	0.02	..	2.99	-	..	..	2.99

- nil or less than 0.005%;
.. data not available.

* ALMP is the sum of the first seven columns.
** PLMP is the sum of the eighth and ninth columns.

a For a note on scope, comparability, the coverage of particular programme categories and participant statistics, see www.oecd.org/els/employmentoutlook/2007.
b No data for Greece, Iceland, Turkey, Japan, Republic of Korea, Mexico or United States.

Source: OECD, 2007a; data extracted 2 Aug. 2007.

Table 7. Participant stocks in LMPs as percentage of the labour force in selected EU transition countries, 2005

Country	Training	Employment incentives	Integration of the disabled	Direct job creation	Start-up incentives	Out-of-work income maintenance and support	Early retirement	ALMP*	PLMP
Bulgaria	0.41[a]	0.42[a]	0.03	1.76[a]	0.06[a]	2.37	-	2.68[a]	2.37
Czech Republic	0.12	0.45	0.31	0.18	0.11	2.68	-	1.16	2.68
Estonia	0.15	0.13	-	0.004[a]	0.004[a]	2.66	-	0.29[a]	2.66
Latvia	0.47	0.14[a]	0.02	0.21	-	2.82[a]	0.42	0.85[a]	2.82[a]
Lithuania	0.34	:	:	0.41	0.01	0.96	0.13	:	1.38
Hungary	0.34	:	-	0.39	0.10	3.08	2.92	:	3.21
Poland	0.65	:	:	0.06	0.02[a]	2.18	-	:	5.10
Romania	0.13	0.64	-	0.24	:	2.50	-	1.01	2.50
Slovakia	0.17	0.59	0.27	4.02	0.42	1.46	0.62	5.47	2.07

- not applicable; : data not available.
* Excludes labour market services.
a Estimated values.

Source: Eurostat, 2007 (data extracted 10 Aug. 2007), author's calculation

Table 8. Participation in LMPs in selected transition countries, 1998
(percentage of average monthly registered unemployment,
if not otherwise stated)

Country	Benefit recipients	Placed with assistance of NES*	Participation in ALMP**	Percentage in:			
				LMT	PW	SE	SE & other
Kazakhstan[a]	60.9		27.9	8.7	8.6	10.6	n.a.
Russian Fed.	89.5	62.6	35.4	16.3	19.1	n.a.	n.a.
Ukraine	53.1	19.2[a]	24.4	12.8	11.6	0.0	0.0

Key: LMT = labour market training; PW = public works; SE = self-employment; SE & other = subsidized employment and other policies.

*   The ratio of placements of registered jobseekers to newly registered unemployment in the course of the year.
**   The ratio of the number of all participants in ALMPs over the year (regardless of the length of participation) to the average monthly number of registered jobseekers in the same year (%).

a   Non-employed jobseekers (registered jobseekers both with and without unemployment status).

Source: O'Leary et al. (2001), p. 33.

Table 9. Participation in training and employment generation programmes
in seven countries in Latin America and the Caribbean, c.1997

Country	Beneficiaries of:			
	Training programmes		Employment generation	
	US$000s	As % of total labour force	US$000s	As % of total labour force
Argentina	133.0	1.4	892.2	9.31
Brazil	740.5	1.6	221.8	0.49
Chile	36.6	0.8	4.3	0.10
Costa Rica	13.1	1.2	8.1	0.71
Jamaica	43.5	4.4	6.0	0.61
Mexico	410.3	1.8	1 024.0	4.42
Peru	1.5	0.1	4.2	0.14

Source: Márquez (1999), p. 11.

Figure 6. Public expenditure on LMPs as percentage of GDP and unemployment rates in selected OECD countries, 2005

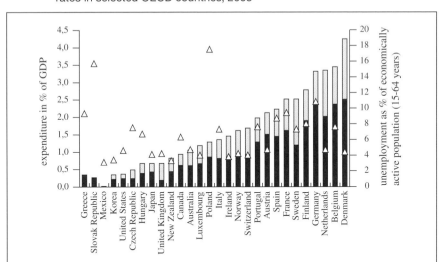

Note: No data for Iceland or Turkey. Sorted by total expenditure.
Source: OECD (2007a), extraction 2007/08/02.

Figure 7. Public expenditure on LMPs per 1% of unemployment in selected OECD countries, 2005

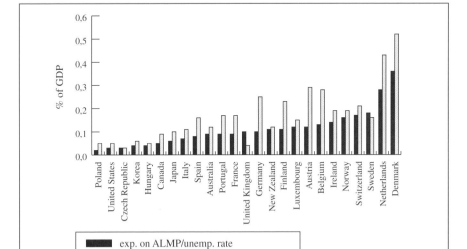

Note: Data incomplete or absent for Greece, Mexico and Slovakia. Sorted by expenditure on ALMPs
Source: OECD (2007a), extraction 2007/08/03.

The next section provides an insight into the importance of specific types of ALMP programmes (public employment services, training, public works, employment subsidies and self-employment) in different regions (OECD, transition countries, Asia – mostly East Asia due to lack of information elsewhere – Latin America and Africa). In the cases where evaluation results are at hand – almost exclusively for OECD countries – they will also be used, in order better to demonstrate the working of different programme types for specific labour market groups. In some regions – especially Africa and Latin America – the choice of programme evidence is severely limited by the lack of relevant information that exists in these regions.

USE AND IMPORTANCE OF ALMP MEASURES IN DIFFERENT REGIONS OF THE WORLD

In many **OECD** countries ALMPs have been used extensively since the economic recession of the mid-1970s. They were given particular prominence in EU Member States in the latter part of the 1990s, not least in response to the EES, which states, for example, that by 2010 25 per cent of the long-term unemployed should be participating in active measures in the form of training, retraining, work experience or other employability measures to match the average of the three most advanced Member States (European Council, 2005). In developing countries, and in the former planned economies where unemployment was barely acknowledged, ALMPs historically have not played a prominent role.

In **transition countries**, as a consequence of the economic restructuring in the early 1990s that brought fundamental changes to the composition of employment by sector and branch, as well as rising unemployment, passive as well as active LMPs have become important policy tools (Nesporova, 1999). They are commonly based on models implemented in advanced OECD countries and were often supported technically as well as financially by the latter. Nevertheless, the unemployment benefit systems of transition countries still tend to be less generous (in duration and replacement rates) than those of advanced OECD countries, and fewer resources are allocated to ALMPs.

In **East Asian** countries, ALMPs were not an important part of the employment policy agenda until the economic crisis in 1997, partly because of low rates of unemployment. However, serious unemployment problems as well as inadequate earnings emerged after the crisis, which increased the potential for using ALMPs. In these countries, ALMP programmes are of particular importance, because unemployment insurance systems either do not exist or have only recently been implemented.[7] Even in countries that have implemented such systems, the large group of informal economy workers is not covered. In the rest of Asia, ALMPs also seem to have gained more prominence since the 1990s.

Latin American countries' experiences with ALMPs have been very different from those of OECD countries, mainly as a result of different labour market circumstances. While OECD countries suffer more from structural unemployment (mismatch between supply and demand), Latin American countries are characterized by high youth and rural unemployment, as well as by the challenges posed by the extensive informal economy. This situation is typical of many developing countries. Because of these different labour market characteristics, in OECD countries ALMPs are more widely used for structural adjustment of labour supply to labour demand (re-skilling through training or retraining, better job matching, etc.), while in developing countries they are often geared to compensating for a lack of labour demand (public works, wage subsidies, etc.). In the wake of economic crises, but also to cope with high rates of existing poverty, some large-scale programmes have been enacted, for example in Argentina and Brazil. These usually make benefit payments conditional on participation in work, or – in the case of the Brazilian *bolsa* – of children in education.

As in the other developing or emerging countries, in **Africa** the informal economy plays a prominent role in job creation. African labour markets are typically characterized by low employment growth in the formal economy coupled with retrenchment of workers, as a by-product of structural adjustment programmes imposed by the IMF and the World Bank. Both contribute to further growth of the informal economy, which becomes the last resort for absorbing labour (ILO, 2000). Here, implementing policies that help to increase self-employment, especially through micro-credit lending, has been of vital importance. In addition, intensive public works programmes have provided employment opportunities in Africa to a vast degree (Devereux, 2002).

In all regions of the developing world, but especially in Africa, it is difficult to come by data on ALMPs. This is in part because many public works programmes are not considered ALMPs, although they provide work and income for the unemployed and underemployed.

Public employment services

Public employment services (PES) in the **OECD** countries fulfil three basic functions: job matching, including career guidance and job search techniques; the management of unemployment benefits; and the referral of jobseekers to reintegration programmes. In recent years, some important changes regarding priority setting as well as functioning of PES have taken place. In a considerable number of OECD countries there has lately been a strong service orientation towards both employees and employers. Technical developments are leading to a growing weight of self-service facilities: vacancy data banks are an essential feature of PES today and data banks of jobseekers' curriculum vitae are becoming more and more significant. One of the targets of the EES is to provide EU-wide access to all union members' job data banks.

New trends in OECD countries include the setting up of one-stop shops, which pool various public services and agencies into a comprehensive strategy that relies on effective cooperation between placement activities and the management of unemployment, as well as social benefits. In this context, the trend towards stronger activation of benefits should be mentioned. Slogans such as "welfare-to-work" or "work-first" depict a policy giving priority to active over passive measures. This trend is especially visible in, for example, Denmark (extensive activation policies) and the United Kingdom (New Deal). For the EU, the Luxembourg Guidelines state that unemployed adults should be given a new start through participation in active programmes before 12 months of unemployment, and youth before six months.

Other ways of enacting the "work-first" strategies are a tightening of eligibility criteria for benefit receipt, as well as a stronger focus on the principle of rights and duties that is often enforced through benefit sanctions. In many countries individually tailored action plans are set up in the employment offices that state the rights as well as the duties of the unemployed. In order to target costly active measures better, profiling techniques have been introduced in a number of OECD countries. Two other recent trends are the decentralization of services, which are often coupled with greater social partner involvement, and the contracting out of certain services, such as training.[8]

The 1990s saw liberalization of the restrictions on private placement offices in many OECD countries, but only Australia and the Netherlands have so far made extensive use of contracting out PES services to private agents (OECD, 2005a, pp. 211-14). PES activities are especially important for the hard-to-place because private agents are more likely to "cream off" candidates (i.e. select those clients who are easier to place).[9]

Since unemployment officially did not exist in planned economy countries, there was no need for public employment services.[10] But with economic transformation and the subsequent rise in unemployment, employment services were set up in **transition countries** based on the models that seemed to have worked in OECD countries, and with financial and logistical help from Western countries and international organizations.

PES in transition countries consist of central labour offices at the national level and a network of offices at the regional and local levels. As in the OECD countries with a long tradition of PES, they are responsible not only for administering unemployment benefits but also for job mediation and implementation of LMPs.

The effectiveness and impact of PES differ from country to country. PES in Central European countries such as Slovenia and Croatia are more advanced on account of the countries' more favourable economic situation, which allows higher investment in staff, equipment and also sophisticated electronic labour market information systems. In contrast, the Southeast European countries are faced with more serious problems. Funding is inadequate, which results in a high turnover of staff, who are usually less motivated, and in services that are restricted to basic functions such as registration of the unemployed, payment of benefits and very limited job matching.[11]

In the five **East Asian** countries that are examined by Betcherman et al. (2001) – Indonesia, the Republic of Korea, Malaysia, the Philippines and Thailand – PES exist but differ markedly from those in industrialized countries.[12] This is mainly due to the lack of unemployment insurance (except for the Republic of Korea) and of established LMPs and labour market information. The economic crisis of the late 1990s resulted in different strategies in the countries observed. In the Republic of Korea and the Philippines one-stop shops were set up, where jobseekers could have access to unemployment benefits (only Korea) or receive job search assistance and vocational training guidance (both countries). Malaysia introduced registration and placement services as well as job fairs for retrenched workers, while Indonesia and Thailand did not launch any new measures. In some countries, there has also been an increase in the activities of regional committees, task forces and governments, as well as tripartite bodies with regard to employment policies (Betcherman et al., 2001).

Other **Asian** countries such as **China** or **India** also have public employment services. These usually operate at local level, while regulations and guidelines are defined centrally. There is only very sparse information on the functioning of PES in these two countries. In China, the unemployment insurance regulations state that unemployment benefits shall be closely incorporated with such employment services as vocational guidance, employment training and self-employment advice. In Shanghai, for example, training centres are attached to the placement centres, thereby assigning PES a wider function than merely registering the unemployed and paying out unemployment benefits. In the context of developing countries, employment services cover by definition only those unemployed people who are registered with the employment offices. The problem of the masses of informally employed/unemployed thus remains a major challenge in these countries.

In a number of Asian countries, private employment services have begun to play a more important role. In countries such as the Philippines, Indonesia and Thailand they have been especially active in transferring local workers to overseas labour markets. There has been strong evidence, however, of severe malpractice by some of these private agents (indebtedness of clients, luring into prostitution, etc.). In order to counter these activities, much stronger regulations have now been established for the registration and admission of private employment agencies (Lim and Sziraczki, 1995, pp. 54 ff.).

PES in **Latin American countries** are usually administered either by the ministry of labour or via national training institutes. As in other developing countries, employment services are less extensive than in OECD countries, the public investment level is lower and PES gained a reputation for offering only the least skilled jobs (Mazza, 2003, pp. 165-66). Furthermore, given that most countries in the region do not have unemployment insurance systems, saving money by getting the unemployed into jobs is not a prime objective of PES reforms. Those countries that do have unemployment insurance often do not use the employment services to administer it. According to Mazza (2003, pp. 166-67), recent reforms of PES in Latin America and the Caribbean have focused on introducing and improving information systems through the use of new technologies,[13] expanding the role of the private and not-for-profit sector, and improving performance through decentralization, more comprehensive services and new assessment tools.[14] In those countries where they do exist (Argentina, Brazil, Chile and Uruguay), unemployment insurance schemes usually have a limited coverage, in part because of the large informal sector. Severance pay, which has a longer tradition in this region, usually represents a greater financial compensation than unemployment insurance (Mazza, 2000, p. 6).[15]

In English-speaking **Africa**, PES have been operating on a very low level of human and fiscal resources.[16] Services are usually at a minimum standard; most PES offices offer only registration services and perform poorly in their traditional placement functions. Being mostly marginalized in low-priority ministries, they face tight budgetary constraints and have even ceased to exist in some places. PES are usually understaffed. Although staff are typically well trained, they lack the necessary tools to perform their work efficiently. Compared to the fast-growing labour force, very few job vacancies are available; registration of job vacancies at the PES is either not mandatory or not enforced. The insufficient capacity of PES and their related infrastructure hampers the design and implementation of LMPs that could help to adjust the workforce through training and similar measures. In addition, PES are disconnected from the informal economy, which is usually the fastest-growing segment. Thus, potential job opportunities in this part of the economy are ignored and PES are hardly accessible for jobseekers in the informal economy.

It seems that some problems with labour market institutions are similar throughout all the regions. A major problem is the need for a coherent and coordinated system of labour market intermediation. Reliable information on supply as well as demand is a prerequisite for good job matching. There are often no requirements for employers to report employment openings to the public employment agencies. As the reputation of PES among employers as well as employees is often bad, better promotion would therefore be necessary. In OECD countries, many new trends can be observed, some of which have already been taken up by a few transition and developing countries (decentralization, profiling, etc.). Attempts at disbursing the functions of PES in developing countries, especially in Africa, often fail because of a severe lack of financial, organizational and technological capacity.

Training

Lifelong learning and training are seen as an important component of strategies to overcome high and persistent unemployment and to adapt the labour force to changing labour market demands in **OECD countries**. The OECD Jobs Strategy, for instance, postulates well-designed, small-scale and carefully targeted training programmes, but it also stresses that during programme participation availability for work should continue and that participation in training should not re-establish benefit entitlements (OECD, 1996, pp. 43-46). Similarly, guideline 23 of the EES calls for expanded and improved investment in human capital, among other means through efficient lifelong learning strategies for all – but especially the low-skilled and older workers – including appropriate incentives and cost-sharing mechanisms (European Council, 2005).

In many EU countries there are contractual and statutory rights to paid time off for training, and in the late 1990s some countries introduced a measure called "job rotation". While giving employed workers time off for education purposes, this measure replaces their post for the duration of their training by an unemployed person who thus gets an opportunity to train on the job. Therefore, job rotation satisfies the training needs of the employed as well as the unemployed. [17] Most evaluation studies on training conclude that job rotation supports the reintegration of the unemployed into the labour market, seems to shorten the unemployment spell and is usually more successful when implemented at an early phase of unemployment (Schmid, 1996, pp. 770ff.). Despite such positive evaluation, job rotation remains small-scale and has even been discontinued in some countries.

A problem in **OECD** countries is the high selectivity of training, especially of further training, for example by age, sex and level of education. [18] This selectivity leads to the paradox that individuals who already have higher levels of education are privileged when it comes to further upgrading of skills.

In **transition economies**, such as Hungary, the Russian Federation and Ukraine, labour market training is commonly employed by countries with high levels of structural unemployment and skill mismatching. Training and retraining are usually provided free of charge to those people registered at the PES. Some countries (Croatia, the Czech Republic, Hungary and Slovenia) also allocate retraining subsidies to employed workers who are likely to become redundant, in order to preserve their jobs, and to ease their intra-company mobility or redeployment. In many other transition countries, however, the legal framework does not allow PES to run programmes for employed workers. Retraining measures are often cofinanced by the firm or the worker. Unemployed persons in training usually receive a stipend that is slightly higher than the unemployment benefit in order to motivate them to participate (O'Leary et al., 2001, p. 26). Measured by their ability to contribute to re-employment, training measures seem to be rather successful. In most transition countries labour market training is the only programme that is regularly monitored regarding re-employment after completion. In the Russian Federation, the average annual placement rate after completion of training was 89 per cent in 1998, and in the Czech Republic it was on average 71 per cent over the period 1991-97, whereas in Poland and Estonia approximately 50 per cent of all training participants found jobs in 1997. The available figures for Hungary indicate that individual training resulted in a higher placement rate (51.3 per cent) than group training (45.6 per cent) in 1997. Re-employment after training in Bulgaria was comparatively low, with an average placement rate of only 35 per cent in 1999 (O'Leary et al., 2001, p. 36; Nesporova, 1999, pp. 59 ff).

The paucity of sound evaluation studies on training in transition countries is a problem. The lack of sufficient data does not allow comparisons of integration results between persons participating in training and those not participating. A noteworthy exception is the evaluation study covering Hungary and Poland by O'Leary, Kolodziejczyk and Lázár (1998). The authors estimated that individual retraining in Hungary and retraining in Poland increased hiring in non-subsidized work by 11 per cent and 12 per cent, respectively (O'Leary et al., 1998, pp. 334-37). Data on the sustainability of jobs that were entered after participating in training measures are not available.

Labour market training has become increasingly popular in the **Asian countries**.[19] The long-term industrial development path of these countries requires a labour force with higher skills, and a number of countries (Indonesia, Malaysia, the Philippines, Singapore, Thailand) have been addressing this need by helping people to adapt to these new skill demands through training measures. In the East Asian countries, the increase in unemployment following the crisis of the late 1990s has shifted the focus of training from general skills upgrading to the reintegration of laid-off workers into the labour market. In the Republic of Korea, for example, participation in vocational training programmes for the unemployed increased eightfold in the wake of the crisis. The two main problems associated with training programmes in East Asia are also characteristic of many other developing countries: first, there is a lack of coordination between various government institutions that are responsible for vocational training and education; and second, there is insufficient communication and feedback between changing labour demand and training design. A recent report on Indonesia showed, for example, that there are 19 different departments involved in over 800 vocational training programmes. In the Philippines and Thailand, there are three separate government agencies with overlapping responsibilities for training activities. As in most developing countries, illiteracy poses a serious problem in many Asian countries, and training must thus often be of a more general nature. Rural children and youth are especially faced with a lack of accessible or affordable schools. Deficient education prevents youth from finding jobs, with girls and young women especially disadvantaged.[20] Their educational attainment opportunities are limited owing to prevailing traditional values, and their literacy level and social status thus remain inferior to that of their male counterparts, setting a further barrier to their employment and income opportunities.

When it comes to the implementation of training programmes, it is necessary to pay special attention not only to women's integration and youth employment concerns but also to the needs of minority groups such as workers with disabilities and those in the informal economy. In most Asian countries, non-governmental organizations (NGOs) have played a vital role in providing non-formal education, for example in agriculture with a special focus on women. In recent years a shift of programmes towards an emphasis of non-farming income resources can also be observed.[21] A problem, however, is that training is often concentrated on traditional female activities. Gender-disaggregated data would be a prerequisite for carefully planned and adapted training activities, but it is often lacking. Although training and education are still inadequate considering the high demand, it is nevertheless improving in Asia. One strategy towards successful training, especially of rural women, is the building up of partnerships between government institutions, NGOs and the private sector.

Starting in the 1980s but mainly in the 1990s, the system of training in **Latin America** has been considerably altered (see especially ILO, 2000b). Previously, training was for the most part centrally organized by a public or, in the case of Brazil, a private body.[22] In some cases (Brazil, Peru, Mexico) it was managed by corporate organizations. In Argentina and Uruguay, vocational training was included in the structure of regular education but without becoming mainstream. The schemes were financed from a specific levy on payrolls. Current trends in training delivery include a greater involvement of the social partners, modernization of delivery, growing private training offers and greater use of communications technology and distance learning. Another trend is skill certification, which makes acquired skills more portable and gives potential employers information they need (Márquez, 2002, p. 11). Two factors have played a decisive role in inducing the reforms: first, the necessity to adapt the training structures to the rising skill demand that emerged because of the internationalization of trade, technological change and the growing flexibility of labour; and, second, critical voices from trade unions and employers' organizations on the management of national training bodies. Previously, training and its financing had been seen as a minor activity mainly because of the relative stability of technology and work tasks, and was therefore in limited demand.

Currently, a host of actors is involved in training in all Latin American countries and the national vocational training institutions are therefore ceasing to be leading players in the supply of training. Ministries of labour, employers and labour organizations, as well as private training agents, have entered the field. The competitive situation among multiple actors favours flexibility and efficiency. On the other hand, it can lead to disadvantages for weaker segments of the labour market and might be too strongly oriented towards the immediate needs of firms, which can be adverse to the pursuit of long-term needs. Here, the government has to provide guidelines, quality standards, control measures and incentives, as well as special offers for disadvantaged labour market groups. A stronger application of evaluation instruments used to assess training results can already be observed. Another challenge is to prevent the diversification of training offers from generating fragmentation.

The variety of regional training experiences is vast. In some countries (for example, in Bolivia, Ecuador, El Salvador, Guatemala and Peru) the responsibility for defining policies and implementing training actions is concentrated in one body. In other countries, at least two bodies coexist: a specialized body, usually the labour ministry, defines policies and strategies, while the implementation of training measures is carried out by multiple agents, among them national or sectoral training institutions (Brazil, Mexico, Uruguay). In Argentina and Chile, the definition but not the implementation of training policies takes place through specialized bodies belonging to the labour ministries, while a large number of agencies and players are responsible for the implementation process. With the upsurge in training offers through private training bodies, the expansion of training in firms, as well as training activities by NGOs promising new financing strategies, are emerging. Alliances between the state and private or intermediary agents are being set up. There is a diversification of state agents in financing (the ministry of education, the ministry of labour and the ministry of social welfare often also intervene) and there are also more private resources through greater participation by firms as investors or implementing agents, as well as individuals.[23] A recent trend in Latin America is the devolution of occupational training to local agents. Implemented and managed at the local level, training content can be better adapted to local needs – local actors' involvement is often an important asset (ILO, 2002b).

In **Africa**, it appears that the popularity of integrated programmes, which combine training with work experience, is increasing. The integration of formal training with entrepreneurship development and enterprise promotion is especially widespread (ILO, 2000, p. 33; Kanyenze et al., 2000, p. 23). In fact, many developing countries are reforming their training systems so that they conform better to general labour market demand, and particularly private sector demand. Training strategies have been widely adapted to the needs of the formal economy, ignoring the massive informal economy in these countries. However, there are some positive changes. Reform measures range from specific small-scale interventions to an overhaul of the educational and training system in terms of institutional structure, organization and content of the course. Examples for such far-reaching restructuring processes are Zambia and Egypt (Kanyenze et al., 2000, pp. 24 ff.).

As in other regions, in Africa youth unemployment rates tend to be notably higher than adult rates. While there is a broad recognition of the importance of formal schooling and the improvement of quality standards, as well as attendance levels, there is little evidence that job-training schemes yield good results. This stems from the fact that they are usually biased towards preparation for formal economy jobs which often do not exist on an adequate scale. Programmes that help to slow the flow from the rural areas to the cities are regarded as especially important (ILO, 2000, pp. 34-35). In the North African countries, education and training are usually centralized, the regional or local authorities have limited control and the private sector has only a marginal role and input in the training process. A lack of legal and statutory regulations further hinders the participation of the private sector (Handoussa and Tzannatos, 2002, pp. 10-11). In North Africa, owing to outdated curricula, which in the absence of evaluation systems are only rarely adapted to new developments, people who complete vocational training are often not well prepared for the skills that are required in the labour market.

In developed as well as developing countries, labour market training has been playing an important role, and in some countries its importance has increased even further in recent years. While in OECD countries the concept of lifelong learning is currently high on the agenda, in developing countries more prominence is given to short-term measures satisfying the urgent needs of upgrading basic skills and education. A common trend is the targeting of measures towards special labour market groups such as the young unemployed, women and other disadvantaged groups. In OECD as well as in developing countries, this often takes place through specialized programmes which take into account the particular needs and constraints of the specific target group. In developing countries, programmes are often initiated by development organizations or through bilateral aid. Paradoxically, in-firm training normally serves the labour market groups that are already advantaged and can thus exacerbate segmentation of the labour market. It is widely recognized that training in the real work context is more useful than classroom training. This knowledge has often been incorporated into the programme design by directly involving possible employers in the training measures (for example, the youth programmes in Chile and Argentina).

In many countries, a movement towards the privatization of training services can be observed. It is generally accepted, however, that state interventions are needed to serve the interests of disadvantaged groups which risk being discriminated against by private training agencies. Some developing countries have proved that, through innovative programmes (for example, the Padhna-Badhna Abhiyan scheme in India) it is possible to achieve success in spreading especially basic skills, even in the absence of ample financial means. While evaluation of the effects of training in OECD countries, and increasingly also in transition countries, is part of the programme, in developing countries sufficient means for more detailed evaluation of programmes' successes and shortcomings are usually lacking. A lack of data often makes it impossible to adjust the programmes to changing labour market needs. In general, if training programmes are designed and implemented in developing countries, special attention should be given to the role of the informal economy. In all regions, it is important that the training content closely matches labour market demands in order to improve the participants' chances of integration into the labour market at the end of the programme. While in developing countries there is a strong focus on youth when it comes to training, in developed countries a growing number of skills training programmes are set up in order to keep older workers in the labour market and to counteract the intensifying financial problems that face social security systems because of a decreasing active labour force in relation to retired workers.

Public works

The goal of direct job creation in **OECD** countries is to increase the available number of jobs in order to compensate for shortcomings in private sector job creation. Direct job creation usually takes place in the public or non-profit sector and is mainly financed by public means. The jobs created are supposed to be additional to existing employment, and to be ones that would not have been created in the absence of the public works programme (Erhel et al., 1996, p. 293). As a general rule, the jobs created should be beneficial to society. They are thus for the most part established in the cultural, environmental or social fields, and are usually of limited duration. In the OECD, public works programmes were especially used throughout the 1970s and early 1980s. At that time, significant numbers of hard-to-place persons were participating in public works. Since then, most of these programmes have been abolished or significantly scaled down, mainly because of negative evaluation results. The public works programmes that still exist are mostly targeted to the long-term unemployed and other disadvantaged labour market groups. In countries with severe unemployment problems, such as Germany after reunification, and in France, these schemes have been used to compensate for a lack of demand and have also served those considered fully employable (Erhel et al., 1996, p. 293).

The extensive placing of the unemployed with strong re-employment problems in public employment programmes risks locking them into a long-term, publicly financed, secondary-track labour market with few possibilities of transition to regular employment. The OECD Jobs Strategy is very critical of public works programmes and suggests using them mainly as work tests and, in case of scarce aggregate demand, as a means of helping the unemployed to maintain contact with the labour market. They should be of short duration and not become a disguised form of permanent employment (OECD, 1996, pp. 11-12). The evaluation results for direct job-creation programmes are mixed. In Finland as well as in the United States, small positive results were reported. An early evaluation study of the German ABM programme showed a significant increase in the outflow of short-term unemployment but no significant effect on long-term unemployment. Similar studies in the United Kingdom did not show any significant outflow impact on any duration category, while in the Netherlands substitution effects as well as deadweight effects were found (OECD, 1993, pp. 66-67).

The choice of public works in **transition countries** appears to be in line with their special labour market problems and needs.[24] Countries with high long-term unemployment, for example, commonly resort to public works programmes to alleviate poverty among this group of the unemployed and to ensure that they do not get disconnected from the labour market. Bulgaria, Hungary, the Russian Federation and Ukraine are among the countries that deploy public works schemes more extensively than others. In remedying the problems associated with the temporary and low-skilled nature of public works, some countries are launching policies to extend the schemes to include jobs requiring higher skills or to link them to training with possibilities for regular or permanent employment after the scheme ends (e.g. Hungary and Slovenia). In some countries (Hungary and Ukraine) public works programmes have been combined with large-scale infrastructure or ecological programmes. Older jobseekers usually have a higher share in these programmes than in other ALMP programmes. This is especially due to their over-representation in long-term unemployment (Fortuny et al., 2003, p. 43).

However, the relative popularity of public works in transition countries does not appear to be justified in terms of their direct employment effects.

According to evaluation studies, no more than 10 per cent of participants find a regular job after finishing the programme (O'Leary et al., 2001, p. 35). Compared to other ALMPs, especially training, public works generate poor integration results. Nevertheless, as they usually involve important infrastructural and community service work, public works are of high value as a tool of economic development.

While in industrialized countries public works projects are often used as a "last resort" measure, in developing countries, where unemployment and particularly poverty are more pronounced, public works are not only useful to provide temporary employment and compensation for the needy but are also important ways of achieving infrastructure development and of promoting the advancement of technical and management skills. In their function as a means of improving transportation, communication and other infrastructure, they also contribute to facilitating agricultural work and marketing (Lim and Sziraczki, 1995, p. 53).

In **East Asia**, public works appear to be the most common ALMP. They are usually implemented more for social relief purposes than for employment development. After the 1997 crisis, the number of public works programmes increased substantially in the five countries examined by Betcherman et al. (2001). In the Republic of Korea, for example, they served around 70 per cent of the country's 1.7 million unemployed in 1999. Public works programmes are especially important in securing income in the absence of unemployment insurance – except for the Republic of Korea, where unemployment insurance beneficiaries are not allowed to participate – and are less costly than other programmes, such as employment subsidies. Despite their positive impact in generating income for the unemployed and their families, these measures have at the same time suffered from various design flaws limiting their effectiveness.

In the case of Indonesia, there was a lack of conceptual clarity about objectives and beneficiaries. In Indonesia, the Republic of Korea and the Philippines, wages were not set at a level that allowed the target group to be reached, while in Thailand, lack of coordination and subsequent overlap led to inefficiencies. In the Philippines and Thailand monitoring was insufficient to allow appropriate readjustment. In general, participation among women was low, especially due to the high share of activities in construction works. No special programmes for women were implemented (Betcherman et al., 2001, pp. 20-23).

In **Latin American** countries, public works are often regarded as poverty alleviation programmes targeted at the unemployed, designed to secure the material well-being of the poorest unemployed rather than their quick return to non-subsidized work. Direct job creation is comparatively expensive. By implementing public works as early as the mid-1970s, Chile was the first country in this region which made extensive use of direct employment creation in order to counter the strong rise in unemployment after the neo-liberal reforms. In countries such as Argentina, Brazil, Colombia and Mexico, these programmes have been introduced more recently. In Argentina, in response to the severe recession of 2002, a new large-scale job creation programme, the

Programa de Jefes y Jefas de Hogar Desocupados, was established. It is aimed at heads of households with children and among other elements offers cash transfers to the unemployed who do not have access to unemployment insurance (Marshall, 2004). In general, direct job creation provides low-paid jobs, which do not compete with the private sector and are usually of short duration. The low wages and the limited duration of the jobs are supposed to ensure that only needy people participate (De Ferranti et al., 2000, p. 91). One strength of these programmes is that, in contrast to other income replacement programmes, they also reach the unemployed who have formerly worked in the informal economy. In fact, the now discontinued Argentinian Trabajar public works programme, for example, served mainly the poorest section of the population (De Ferranti et al., 2000, p. 95). Similarly, the Mexican Programa de Empleo Temporal, which was launched to tackle the consequences of the 1995 crisis and offers work in community projects, is targeted at the poorest segment of the population in rural areas (Marshall, 2004, pp. 30ff; SEMARNAT, 2007).

Public works in **Africa** are often used in times of emergency such as natural disasters and civil conflicts, but also in a more strategic way during economic downturns. They are operated in almost all countries and mainly provide participants with pay, food or a combination of both in exchange for temporary labour. In some cases, these labour-intensive strategies generate added value through infrastructure development or service development. Labour-based work programmes have gained popularity because, if carefully planned and implemented, they can help to create jobs for the unemployed and underemployed, especially in rural areas. In addition to creating jobs, labour-based technologies usually prove to be less costly than capital-intensive approaches which make excessive use of scarce foreign exchange earnings (Kanyenze et al., 2000, pp. 43-44). Sub-market wage rates are seen as a useful means to target the needy instead of people who are already employed. Since public works programmes have often been characterized by low levels of work organization, low productivity and efficiency, and poor quality of the end product, there is often doubt about the usefulness of integrating labour-intensive work methods into national policies. Public works programmes will only have longer-term employment generation and poverty alleviation effects, however, if they are directly linked to economic growth. It is thus an important task for governments as well as for the international community to support the broad integration of labour-based strategies into public investment policies.

While training usually targets labour supply, policies aiming at creating jobs – and thus targeting labour demand – are of critical importance in countries where effective demand for work is scarce. Consequently, in developing countries direct job-creation activities appear to be the major focus of ALMPs. In these countries, public works programmes – especially through labour-based technologies – not only create employment and thus a living wage for the unemployed and underemployed, but also meet wider economic, social and ecological needs.

In contrast, in **OECD** countries direct job creation through public works is no longer seen as a viable way of strengthening the re-employment opportunities of the unemployed. Indeed, according to the evaluation study results from OECD as well as transition countries, this ALMP measure seems to be the least beneficial in getting unemployed people into regular non-subsidized jobs. Most evaluation studies report minor or no effects on labour market integration, and some even report negative effects due to reduced search intensity. Positive effects can be achieved, however, through careful targeting of public works towards severely disadvantaged groups. It is useful to combine the participation in direct employment creation programmes with additional training components that aim at raising the employability of participants and thus preparing them for the transition to regular employment.

Employment subsidies

Most **OECD** countries use a variety of employment subsidies with differing design features that are closely connected not only to the labour market group they are aimed at, but also to the prevailing welfare system. Employment subsidies usually account for a significant share of ALMP spending; they can either be short term or long term, aimed at the demand side of the labour market by reducing the cost of employment creation or at the supply side by setting incentives for the unemployed to take up employment, or, to put it simply, by "making work pay".

Employment subsidies are usually targeted at disadvantaged labour market groups such as the long-term unemployed, the elderly or single parents. On the demand side, they are supposed to encourage employers to give preference to the disadvantaged segments of the labour market. On the supply side, they try to encourage the target groups to re-enter the labour market by increasing the difference between welfare benefits and low-wage income, and thereby weakening the so-called "benefit trap". Because of additional child benefits under some welfare schemes and the cost of childcare when moving into work, the difference between welfare benefits and wage incomes is usually very small for families with many children, and so this segment is faced with strong disincentives to work. Depending on the welfare system and also on the financing of the social security system, employment subsidies can consist of exemptions from social security or tax payments, directly compensate the employer for a certain percentage of the wage or allow the beneficiaries to keep a part of their welfare benefits in addition to earned wages for a limited time. The duration as well as the amount of the subsidy usually depend on the severity of the beneficiary's labour market disadvantage.

Short-term employment subsidies are used in almost all OECD countries, and there is often a wide variety of programmes depending on the target group. Frequently, the take-up rates by employers are low because of a general unawareness of the existence of these programmes, or high administrative barriers. In order to enhance visibility of these measures, it would be preferable to combine the different schemes and especially promote them among smaller firms (OECD, 2003a, pp. 125-26). Evaluation studies have pointed to different possible negative effects of short-term employment subsidies, namely the substitution effect (displacement of non-subsidized by subsidized persons) and deadweight effect (the job would have been created without the subsidy). In order to control benefit abuse and to ensure participants' subsequent employment, employers in some countries are obliged to keep the employee for a certain period after the subsidy runs out on penalty of subsidy repayment.

Long-term employment subsidies, so-called "in-work benefits", which top up low wages, are used by a smaller number of OECD countries. Some countries, namely, the United States with the Earned Income Tax Credit (EITC), and the United Kingdom with its Working Families' Tax Credit (WFTC), have many years of experience in permanently subsidized low wages. [25] Other countries, for example Belgium and France, have introduced long-term subsidy schemes more recently. In-work benefits are often targeted at specific groups such as long-term welfare recipients, workers with children, single-parent families, or full-time workers with low earnings (OECD, 2005b, pp. 152-54). The amount of subsidy generally declines as wages increase in order to avoid a sudden total withdrawal of benefit when the upper qualifying wage level is passed. In some countries a minimum number of hours is required in order to qualify for wage subsidies. There are different problems related to these long-term schemes. First, the fact that subsidies are paid as long as wages remain below a certain threshold does not encourage beneficiaries to develop their skills (OECD, 2003a, p. 121). Second, if subsidies are paid depending on the household income, spouses' incentives to take up work decline. Third, the introduction of permanent measures to support low-wage jobs is often met with major concern by trade unions. In general, evaluation studies agree that wage subsidies to the private sector are more effective than direct job creation in the public sector. In France, however, the youth unemployment rate was considerably lowered through direct temporary job creation, while a private segment of the same programme was less successful. Evaluation studies also suggest that wage subsidies redistribute employment possibilities to more disadvantaged groups without necessarily creating many more jobs (OECD, 2003a, p. 128).

The importance of subsidized employment varies greatly in the **transition countries**. In the Czech Republic, Hungary and Romania, programmes of this kind have become the most important ALMPs in terms of both expenditure and participation (though there are no data for Hungary on the latter indicator) (Eurostat, 2007). In the CIS countries, on the other hand, they have either been almost entirely discontinued for financial reasons (as in the Russian Federation and Ukraine) or never introduced at all (as in Azerbaijan and Kazakhstan) (Kwiatkowski et al., 2001; O'Leary et al., 2001). During the early 1990s wage subsidies were widely used in the Czech Republic and Slovakia to ease structural change from declining sectors to growing ones and to accelerate the redeployment of workers displaced as a result of the economic transformations of these years. While the Czech Republic ceased implementing large-scale subsidized employment programmes after the initial phases of structural transformation, Slovakia still uses such policies extensively to enhance weak labour demand in crisis regions, as well as to support the initial employment of school-leavers (O'Leary et al., 2001). Special wage subsidy programmes for graduates also exist in Hungary, Poland and Romania, aiming to facilitate the transition from study to employment by awarding subsidies to employers that hire young people who have recently left school or college. Redeployment rates of those who have benefited from subsidized employment programmes in Hungary, and from the so-called "intervention works" in Poland, reached over 50 per cent.

Employment subsidies that provide incentives to employers to maintain existing employment and/or create new jobs are not commonly used in **East Asian** countries. Of the five countries examined by Betcherman et al. (2001), only the Republic of Korea and Malaysia have employment maintenance subsidy programmes. In both countries such measures showed some success. In Malaysia, subsidies are the primary labour market strategy. In China, a number of policies to encourage employers to hire workers from among the long-term unemployed, disabled or other disadvantaged groups have recently been introduced. The policies range from income tax reductions or exemptions, and grants or loans from the unemployment insurance fund, to preferential access to and use of land (Lim and Sziraczki, 1995, p. 52).

Employment subsidies have also been used in some of the **Latin American** countries. Their role here seems to be relatively restricted, though; public works programmes still seem to be more popular in this region than employment subsidies to private firms. In general, most countries in the region invest very few resources in employment generation programmes, and these programmes consequently benefit only a small proportion of the workforce (Márquez, 1999, p. 9). Argentina is an exception to this rule: its large-scale direct employment creation programme, Programa de Jefes y Jefas de Hogar Desocupados, also subsidizes private sector employment. Furthermore, in 2003 the Argentinian ministry of labour announced Más y Mejor Trabajo, an employment subsidy programme with multiple objectives including the reintegration of unemployed workers into the labour market and adaptation of the private sector to new productive processes (Marshall, 2004, p. 31). Some countries, for example Brazil since 2003, focus employment subsidies on young workers in particular (Marshall, 2004, p. 31). Apart from these examples, public works programmes seem to be more popular in this region than employment subsidies to private firms.

Subsidized employment schemes are very rare in **Africa**. Kanyenze et al. (2000, p. 42) state that they are not aware of any such schemes in English-speaking Africa, and there is very little evidence of subsidized employment schemes in French-speaking Africa either. If any such subsidies are allocated to businesses, they usually seem to be targeted at relatively well-educated young people, thus performing a function similar to apprenticeship support. Owing to the predominance of the informal economy, strategies that promote self-employment play a much bigger role in this region than employment promotion in private businesses through subsidies.

An advantage of employment subsidies is that they can be used on the supply side in order to set work incentives and redistribute labour on the demand side. Short-term subsidies are used in almost all OECD countries to improve the situation of disadvantaged labour market groups. While in developed countries wage subsidies are also often used as in-work benefits to compensate for the insignificant differences between welfare benefits and low wages, in developing countries employment subsidies are usually targeted at the demand side so that additional employment will ensure people's well-being in the absence of welfare benefits. In transition countries, the existence of wage subsidies seems to depend on the financial situation of the country: wage subsidies are often targeted to young unemployed or school-leavers to ease the school-to-work transition. Evidence from OECD countries, and to a certain degree also from transition countries, shows that wage subsidies are in general more successful than public works when it comes to employment integration. In addition, they are usually less costly. But country examples also illustrate that the design and the targeting of wage subsidies are crucial to their success. Sound evaluation studies on this subject for other regions are very scarce.

In East Asia, employment subsidies did not play an important role until the crisis of 1997. They have subsequently been introduced in some countries with the aim of preventing massive lay-offs. In the Republic of Korea especially, they have also been targeted to certain disadvantaged labour market groups in order to prevent the spread of poverty. In Latin America, in general, indirect tax rebates seem to prevail over direct subsidies to employers or employees. In African countries, employment subsidies are either non-existent or play only a very marginal role .

Self-employment and micro-enterprise creation

If demand for labour is scarce, subsidies and additional advisory services can also be used to promote self-employment and small enterprises (see e.g. Reinecke and White, 2004). In contrast to most other ALMPs, in **OECD** countries measures of this kind are generally not seen as suitable for the unemployed with severe employment barriers. According to evaluation studies from OECD countries, this type of measure mainly appears to help a special category of the unemployed, namely relatively young men with comparatively high levels of education (Martin, 1998, p. 21). Owing to the possibility of additional job creation within the newly founded firms, self-employment measures have not only direct employment effects but also indirect ones. In order to support additional job creation, some countries subsidize the wages of workers who are taken on by newly self-employed entrepreneurs during a certain time period.

Self-employment initiatives of the unemployed are supported by the PES through different measures. In addition to material help for the start-up, help is given in developing a business idea and in setting up a business plan. The formerly unemployed entrepreneurs can usually rely on their welfare benefits for a fixed time after the firm's creation in order to assure their living subsistence during the transition period. In countries such as Germany, where self-employed persons do not qualify for unemployment benefits, the right to draw on former benefit claims for a certain period is aimed at easing the decision to take up self-employment. In most countries a number of different programmes for self-employment assistance exist at national as well as regional level. Sometimes specific programmes are set up to serve special target groups such as women or young people. Subsidies for self-employment initiatives normally reach less than 5 per cent of the unemployed. According to a study on micro-finance in industrialized countries, the small number of self-employment initiatives among unemployed and formerly unemployed entrepreneurs nevertheless make up a considerable part of the new firm creators – 50 per cent in France, 19 per cent in Germany and 40 per cent in the United Kingdom (ILO, 2002a, p. 45). When it comes to business survival rates, the self-employed coming from unemployment seem to do as well as other self-employed persons. Business survival rates of three years were 53 per cent in France, 70 per cent in Germany and 60 per cent in the United Kingdom for formerly unemployed persons. Survival rates stood at 74 per cent in Ireland after 2.5 years, 61 per cent in the Netherlands after 3.5 years and 57 per cent in the United States after five years (ILO, 2002a, p. 46).

Success of business start-ups depends on the firm's size (the larger the better), location, legal form and financial management. It must also be kept in mind that not all self-employed who give up their businesses go back to relying on welfare benefits: approximately 30 to 40 per cent return to regular dependent employment (ILO, 2002a, p. 41). As in other ALMP measures, deadweight effects of self-employment promotion measures are considerable. According to evaluation studies, 56 per cent of self-employment programme participants in Canada would have created their own businesses eventually without help from the PES. Deadweight effects in Ireland and the United Kingdom amounted to 40-65 per cent and 48-70 per cent respectively. In many cases, self-employment support merely speeded up business creation. The cost-effectiveness of these programmes seems to be reasonable in comparison to other ALMP measures, although studies on this issue lack precision (ILO, 2002a, p. 31).

Even in industrialized countries, the demand for small loans is often not met, especially due to a lack of sufficient collateral among the unemployed. This identifies an opportunity for state, NGO or voluntary sector intervention. In some OECD countries, such as Greece and Italy, initiatives have been under way to facilitate business start-ups by cutting the administrative formalities and costs of setting up a business (OECD, 2002, pp. 127 and 140).

In **transition countries**, in terms of the prevalence and participation success of different active measures, self-employment programmes are still very modest in outreach, although evaluation results show that this kind of measure can be very promising for a highly skilled subgroup of the unemployed (Nesporova, 1999, p. 61). The small take-up and impact of these measures seems to be in accordance with these countries' historical and institutional culture. As pointed out in O'Leary et al. (2001, p. 37), "few people are willing and able to run a business unless they are forced into it". Common problems of transition economies concerning self-employment are a lack of managerial skills, insufficient access to finance due to weak financial systems and poor risk rating of formerly unemployed entrepreneurs, as well as a comparatively hostile business environment. Obtaining financing seems to be the biggest obstacle, although a number of financing schemes have been developed.

There are some examples of labour market programmes promoting self-employment. Slovakia, for example, in response to its comparatively low self-employment rate and the high number of market opportunities associated with self-employment, launched a business promotion programme. Slovakia and Poland are in fact the only EU accession countries where expenditure on start-up incentives is at least equal to the EU-15 average (see table 2). A business promotion programme was also adopted in Kazakhstan, where labour demand in the formal economy is too weak to capture the high numbers of unemployed and underemployed. In 1998, more than one-third of all participants in ALMPs took place in a large-scale self-employment programme. However, the outcome of this programme has been disappointing, as most participants failed to start or sustain a business (O'Leary et al., 2001, p. 37).

As a result of advanced screening of potential beneficiaries, business start-up programmes have become relatively successful in transition countries. High redeployment rates have been achieved, for instance, in Hungary, where 85 per cent of the participants in the business support scheme set up and sustained their own businesses, and in Poland, where 80 per cent of the recipients of a business start-up loan were successful in 1997 (O'Leary et al., 2001, p. 37). A study of the Czech Republic found that wage subsidies for the self-employed had positive employment integration effects but no effects on earnings (Večernik, 2001, p. 57). In Poland, however, according to an evaluation study by O'Leary et al. (1998, pp. 341-3), self-employment through the business start-up scheme resulted in remarkable gains in monthly earnings, in contrast to Hungary. Poland's self-employment programme also achieved better results than the Hungarian programme in indirect job creation: 27 per cent of participants hired at least one other worker, in contrast to 18 per cent in Hungary. An interesting feature of the Polish programme is the business survival incentive that is set by granting a 50 per cent reduction in repayment of loans to those self-employed who stay in business for at least two years. The success of entrepreneurship programmes depends not only on the overall economic situation of the specific country and its openness to business creation, but also on a functioning infrastructure for business and vocational training, financial and technical support, as well as soft support in the form of marketing and counselling (Nesporova, 1999, p. 60). Beside the need to counter the problem of sparse credit possibilities for start-up businesses, another challenge is to help the businesses operating in the informal economy to become legal.

Government support for self-employment and micro-enterprise creation is a significant policy tool in the countries of **East Asia**. Support programmes for entrepreneurs have existed for a long time as part of the overall industrial policy framework of the countries rather than as ALMP tools.

In **Asia**, as in other regions, financing is the most serious obstacle to self-employment and small enterprise development. Access to credit is especially restricted for rural women, not only due to traditionally low levels of trust in the success of women's self-employment activities but also because of their lack of collateral – it is usually men who are in control of productive resources such as land or houses. Many countries in this region have designed programmes, often with bilateral or multilateral help, to increase access to credit for small and medium-sized enterprises (SMEs). Specific programmes for women and other disadvantaged groups exist. The most famous example of a successful micro-credit programme is the Grameen Bank in Bangladesh. Lessons that can be learned from the Grameen Bank experience and other flourishing micro-credit programmes are, among others, that successful credit programmes have certain features in common: new participants are usually only offered small loans; with regular repayment the size of loans available rises; market interest rates should be charged in order to achieve programme sustainability; group lending strategies are useful not only for participant screening but also to avoid the necessity of formal collateral. Placing high importance on the improvement of screening through information sessions, preliminary interviews, training and developing business plans not only reduces deadweight losses but also enhances the businesses' prospects of success (Betcherman and Islam, 2001, p. 307).

According to a World Bank study, SMEs that were participating in micro-credit programmes in the Philippines performed better in many dimensions than their non-participating counterparts, even though the magnitude of the job-creation and poverty-reduction effects appeared minor (World Bank, 1998, quoted in Betcherman and Islam, 2001, p. 336). There are also various assistance programmes in East Asia that provide management training, technological capacity, office space and a range of other services to entrepreneurs (Betcherman and Islam, 2001). A recent study on credit programmes in Indonesia concluded that government intervention fostering the development of an environment conducive to the working and development of commercial financial institutions is the best strategy to serve SMEs (Betcherman and Islam, 2001, p. 336). When it comes to micro-finance, considerable discrimination against women can still be observed, although it is for a large part women who have to ensure household subsistence.

As in other developing countries, micro-finance initiatives play an important role in **Latin America**. Lack of access to credit is one of the main problems faced by micro-, small and medium enterprises in this region (Llisterri, 2006, p. 6). While traditionally credit lending has been performed by non-profit organizations, during the last five years banks in Latin America have expanded financial services to low-income households; indeed, in Venezuela, Brazil and Colombia, policy-makers have compelled banks to enter the micro-finance field (Abate-Franjul, 2006, pp. 1 ff.). In a number of countries governments run programmes to assist micro-enterprises and small firms in both the formal and informal sectors. These programmes are usually targeted at specific business areas and at segments of the population that have limited or no access to formal credits. A good example is the Brazilian Programa de Geração de Emprego, Trabalho e Renda (PROGER), a large government programme that, besides granting credits to micro-enterprises and small firms in rural and urban areas, also offers technical, managerial and professional training and assistance (Marshall, 2004, p. 32; Ministério do Trabalho e Emprego, 2007). [26]

In most **African** countries, a considerable number of local, national and international organizations are involved in programmes and measures that support the take-up or extension of entrepreneurial activities by the unemployed. In this region, youth is the fastest growing segment of the population. Low enrolment rates in school and high drop-out rates lead to large groups of young people who are illiterate and thus stand less chance of succeeding in the formal labour market. Self-employment support and micro-enterprise development strategies in the informal economy are increasingly seen as a possible response to the serious youth unemployment problem in Africa. Projects in this area range from small-scale NGO activities to large-scale nationwide programmes supported not only by the national government but also by international organizations and other donors. In some countries, specific micro-enterprise development programmes exist that are directly targeted to youth, for example the Youth Action Programme in Zambia. In other countries, quotas for the promotion of youth employment are included in the general programmes (Kanyenze et al., 2000, p. 29). Kanyenze et al. (2000) propose that enterprise development targeted at youth should not take place as an isolated activity but should be part of an overall economic restructuring process with the goal of transforming the relationship between formal and non-formal economies, rural farm and non-farm activities, urban and rural sectors, industrial and agricultural sectors, and domestic and international economies.

While evaluation studies in OECD countries and in transition countries have revealed that self-employment programmes cater to the needs of only a specific sub-group of unemployed (highly educated, young and mostly male), and hence are used for only a small percentage of the unemployed, in developing countries micro-enterprise creation programmes are an important policy tool for a broad range of the unemployed. Not only in developing countries but also in developed countries, access to financing for micro-businesses seems to remain the predominant problem. The unemployed often lack sufficient collateral and are frequently regarded as posing bad credit risks. In many developing countries, women are especially discriminated against when it comes to credit granting. To counter these problems, many different strategies have been adopted. Some governments give credit guarantees in order to increase the availability of credit, while others require commercial banks to grant a certain percentage of their credits to SMEs. NGOs and government programmes use donor money or money from institutions such as the World Bank or the International Monetary Fund as additional sources of credit catering to SMEs.

In order to overcome the collateral problem, strategies of group lending are frequently adopted. Another possible way to enhance the chances of credit recovery is the gradual increase of grants to participants depending on former repayment accuracy. Although some general lessons can be learned concerning the design of successful programmes, well-functioning programmes are not easy to copy because their success often depends significantly on the general and policy environments, as well as on traditions. Not only financing but also help on technical and management issues is needed, and a business-friendly environment (reducing set-up costs and time) is also of great importance. While in OECD and transition countries self-employment programmes often aim at transforming work in the informal economy into formal employment, in many developing countries the large informal economy is recognized as a fact and is even incorporated into programme design. There is still much discussion about the appropriate design of micro-credit programmes. Some advocate the minimal approach that mainly grants credits and works towards the self-suffi-ciency of the programme. Others ardently defend the broader but more cost-intensive welfare approach that takes into account the necessity of additional training in order to cater to the needs of more disadvantaged groups. In addi-tion to initial assistance, all self-employment programmes should also follow up closely the development of the businesses created in order to ensure subse-quent financing or technical help should business problems arise. When it comes to programme design, it should be kept in mind that most of the time regionally set up programmes or national programmes with strong regional components prove more successful than centrally run programmes. Programme evaluation remains a prerequisite for success; but, especially in developing countries, money as well as the necessary technical instruments to carry this out thoroughly are usually lacking.

SUMMING UP

It can be concluded from the preceding examples that ALMPs are used in all regions of the world, but the way in which they are used, the importance allocated to different types of ALMPs and the extent to which they are used vary from region to region, though to a lesser degree between countries within a specific region. Table 10 gives a condensed overview of the importance and characteristics of specific ALMP measures in the regions considered here.

Some of the differences in the use and design of ALMPs are related to the type and extent of the unemployment problem. For example, the mere quanti-tative gap between labour supply and labour demand, even leaving aside the informal labour market, is enormous in developing countries. This gap is greater in transition countries than in advanced countries, where quantitative gaps exist, but the quality (structural) dimension (by skills/location) is very important too. This in turn affects the choice of ALMPs: in the absence of suffi-cient demand, measures should focus on the demand side (e.g. direct public

Table 10.   Overview of importance and characteristics of the specific ALMP measures in different regions of the world

ALMP measures	OECD	Transition economies	Asia	Latin America	Africa
PES	+++	++	+	+	+
	Function: Advanced job matching; administration of benefits; referral to active programmes *Trends*: Decentralization; contracting out of certain services; favouring of active over passive measures; profiling; one-stop shops; privatization; employment companies (private for-profit or non-profit-making labour market intermediaries) *Problems*: unclear reforms; absence of best practice model; in some cases overstaffed	Set up in the period of economic transition with help from OECD countries and modelled on their services *Function*: Job mediation; implementation of active measures; administration of benefits *Problems*: Inadequate funding; in some countries limited to only basic functions	Owing to a lack of unemployment benefits in most East Asian countries, the function of benefit administration is not applicable Advances in most East Asian countries following the crisis *Trends*: One-stop centres; growing impact of private employment services (recently stronger regulation of these because of examples of malpractice)	Minimal operation before the 1990s Efforts to modernize the services in the 1990s; some progress achieved *Problems*: PES are often understaffed and staff frequently lack adequate skills	Often available but operate at a very low level of fiscal and human resources (low priority is given to them) Minimum-standard services; often only formal registration of jobseekers without any services *Problems*: Although staff are often skilled, serious lack of necessary material and tools; generally low registration of job vacancies; hardly accessible for informal economy workers
Training	+++	++	++	++	++
	Function: provide employability to jobless workers; also labour market training for the employed Despite bleak evaluation record, prevailing ALMP measure in the EU *Problems*: Uncertain results; high selectivity, especially for further training towards the more privileged labour market segments *Trends*: emphasis on lifelong learning	In most countries, not most important measure in terms of either expenditure or participation More successful than in developed countries Typically free of charge for persons registered at the PES; the stipend is usually slightly higher than passive unemployment benefit *Problems*: In many countries PES cannot run preventive programmes for the employed, even if they are in danger of losing their jobs	Increasing popularity of training measures; need to help people adapt to the new skill demands; in some East Asian countries sharp increase in training measures in the wake of the crisis Often has to address deficiencies in basic education rather than further training *Problems*: Lack of sufficient adaptation of training design to changing labour demand; lack of coordination between institutions *Trends*: Focus on women by NGOs; shift of programmes towards non-farming income activities	Before 1990s, generally centrally organized. Currently, greater involvement of social partners, growing private training offers, modernization of delivery *Problems*: Plurality of actors can lead to disadvantages for weaker labour market segments *Trends*: Stronger application of evaluation; expansion of training in firms; more private resources; referral of occupational training to local bodies	Growing popularity of integrated programmes combining training with work experience (especially entrepreneurship) Some positive changes due to reforms (in some countries far-reaching restructuring processes of the training system) *Problems*: Biased towards formal economy jobs; only limited role of local authorities and marginal role of private sector; outdated curricula *Trends*: More participatory approaches, more programmes targeted to women

Table 10. (Cont.)

ALMP measures	OECD	Transition economies	Asia	Latin America	Africa
Public works/ direct job creation	+ Extensively used up to the 1980s; in the 1990s more rarely used due to negative evaluation results Almost exclusively targeted to the hard-to-place and long-term unemployed or youth (except for situations with severe unemployment problems, e.g. eastern Germany after reunification) *Problems:* Risk of trapping people in secondary labour markets *Trends:* Use a work text; combination with training	++ In some countries extensive use, especially those with high long-term unemployment (to avoid disconnection from the labour market) Important for infrastructure and community development *Problems:* Poor integration and earnings results for participants *Trends:* Extending schemes to include jobs with higher skills; integrating training	+++ Important means for infrastructure development and advancement of skills; multiplier effects by facilitating agricultural work and marketing through improved infrastructure Use of this measure in East Asia increased substantially in the aftermath of the crisis as a social relief measure in the absence of unemployment benefits *Problems:* Design flaws; lack of coordination; insufficient monitoring	++ Targeted poverty alleviation programmes *Problems:* Often short-lived programmes; funding problems; difficult to organize work *Trends:* Targeting of programmes to unemployed heads of family	+++ Often used in times of emergency (natural disaster; civil conflicts) but also more strategically during economic downturns Available in almost all countries; targeted to the needy through use of sub-market wages *Function:* Providing pay, food or a combination of both to needy participants; often used in infrastructure development (multiplier effects) *Trends:* Growing popularity of labour-based infrastructure approaches (in addition to employment generation; less costly than conventional approaches and saving of foreign exchange earnings
Employment subsidies	+++ Account for a significant share of ALMP spending; more frequent use of short-term rather than long-term subsidies; the latter set incentives to take low-wage jobs *Problems:* Short-term subsidies: substitution and deadweight effects; often low take-up by especially smaller firms due to administrative barriers. Long-term subsidies: manifestation of low-wage jobs; discouragement of skills development	++ Varying importance. Should ease structural change from declining sectors to growing ones, accelerate the redeployment of displaced workers, but evaluation usually shows negative results. *Trends:* Increasingly used to ease the school-to-work transition for young people	+ Not commonly used or only recently introduced. Compensation programme (e.g. for elderly in the absence of regular pension rights or preferred to passive unemployment benefits) *Problems:* Uncertain results; distortion of labour markets because of low wages; no information on programmes; administrative rules too complex	+ Minor importance; few resources, therefore only small fractions of the workforce are involved *Trends:* Indirect tax rebates prevail over direct subsidies to employers	+ Insignificant; if available, then very small-scale and usually targeted to young people

59

Table 10. (Cont.)

ALMP measures	OECD	Transition economies	Asia	Latin America	Africa
Self-employment	+	+	++	++	++
	Suited to a specific category of unemployed (younger, better-educated, male)	Still very modest in outreach, although financial as well as technical help for business creation has been allocated by EU (to accession countries) and evaluation results are generally favourable for specific subgroups of the unemployed	Significant policy tool; entrepreneurial programmes have existed for a long time as part of the overall industrial policy framework	High importance of micro- and small enterprises.	Variety of measures in support of micro-enterprise creation (organized by NGOs and international organizations as well as national governments), often targeted to young people (serious labour market integration problems)
	Often also support of additional job creation by self-employed	*Problems*: General lack of managerial skills; insufficient access to finance; comparatively hostile business environment	*Problems*: Access to credit; formerly also discrimination against women (today programmes are often targeted directly at women or young people)	In some countries government supports micro-enterprise development credits, counselling and training	*Trends*: Enterprise development strategies in the informal economy; decentralization of implementation
	Problems: high deadweight losses; demand for small loans is often not met for lack of collateral; access to credit and business support often difficult	*Trends*: Help to businesses operating in the informal economy to become legal.		*Problems*: Although many programmes exist, take-up by SMEs is often low due to high costs of services	

+++ very important in region;   ++ of moderate importance;   + not important.

60

job creation, employment subsidies, enterprise creation schemes). Successful policies often integrate both the supply and demand sides in the design of ALMPs (e.g. training in public works, training for entrepreneurs, subsidies with training requirements). Focusing exclusively on the supply side incurs the risk of preparing the unemployed for jobs that are non-existent. Qualification upgrading through training of the unemployed can be helpful in the absence of jobs, in order to ensure that the unemployed remain prepared for the time when the labour market situation recovers. When it comes to training, it is important to offer measures that respond to the abilities and skills required by the market; in many OECD countries forecasting instruments have been set up in recent years that try to predict which sectors or jobs will grow and decline in both the short and the long term. However, experience has shown that predictions are usually poor and/or not followed by the training system.

Differences in the choice of policy instruments also stem in part from differences in the organization and strength of the delivery institutions. While all countries are currently trying to set up or enhance labour market institutions such as employment services, unemployment insurance systems, labour market information systems and ALMPs, these institutions are as yet rather ineffective when it comes to job matching, benefit administration or ALMP implementation. A major reason for inadequate measures and malfunctioning delivery institutions is the absence of sufficient funding. However, even where funding exists, other reasons for ineffectiveness are of an organizational, administrative and political nature. A combination of the following can lead to ineffectiveness: poor design of institutions; involvement of a multitude of different institutions (e.g. ministries), and poor or absent coordination between them, resulting in overlapping and uncertain competencies; the absence of social partner involvement; no long-term planning; no or failed decentralization. In order to counter these problems and to create and implement ALMP measures that are well adapted to prevailing needs, it is very important that evaluation research be carried out. Only through labour market policy evaluation can the effects of programme participation on participants and the economy in general truly be assessed. Chapter 7 takes a closer look at evaluation efforts in different countries.

Table 11 gives a checklist of problems and solutions in the area of ALMPs that countries have enacted, as well as some additional ideas on solutions. It does not discriminate between regions and countries, but considers problems that are affecting all countries using these types of programmes to different degrees. However, while problems might often be similar, solutions will depend on a variety of conditions that may or may not exist, such as sufficient funding, efficient institutions to handle programmes, organizational capacities, etc.

Table 11.   Active labour market policies: Problems and possible solutions

Problems	Various solutions sought by countries	Additional ideas
Employment services		
General:	*General:*	*General:*
Administering rather than serving the unemployed; being remote from market needs; centralized structures	Move from bureaucratic rules and segmented services to results-based and client-oriented integrated labour market services. By establishing either enhance public services, or public/private partnerships or via privatization, make employment services user-friendly through self-service, personalized services and one-stop shops, and adapt to local needs through decentralization	Conceive the whole matching process in terms of labour market inter-mediation; add coherence to the institutions in place by allocating clear functions to each element from job-broking to placing people in labour market measures
		Create either integrated services or an overview body for the whole labour market intermediation structure, for example in labour ministry with social partners, but also on decentralized levels
		Monitor reforms but leave "incubation" time for changes to take place. Superposing reform after reform might result in inefficiencies
Specific:	*Specific:*	
Low vacancy reporting	Employer prospecting	
Low market share	Employer prospecting/self-service/computerization (job banks)	
Bad matching of:		
unemployed to jobs	Profiling of unemployed/individual services for employability	
unemployed to measures	Profiling of unemployed and referral to adequate remedial measures/effective labour market policy measure for employability	
Gender biases	Specific efforts for placement of women	

Table 11.   (Cont.)

Problems	Various solutions sought by countries	Additional ideas
Training		
General:	*General:*	*General:*
Insufficient levels; mismatch between market demand and training; complex and overlapping structure of delivery; low level of social partner involvement; insufficient planning; bad image of labour market training for the unemployed; lifelong learning a mere slogan	Create training culture and awareness of different types of education and training, and their relationships (between basic and further education, and initial and further vocational training) and establish concrete plans for different groups; profiling of unemployed according to training needs for lifelong learning at several stages in professional life; let the industry parties determine training needs and how to respond to them; monitor and evaluate	Modular training with possibility of combining a number of short-term modules into valid certification; give new impetus to mixed types of training (work, education and training institutions). Gather knowledge from various sources to establish scenarios on development paths and different training needs
Specific:	*Specific:*	*Specific:*
Unclear knowledge of training needs	Needs assessment, labour market information systems	Use local knowledge
Compensation for schooling rather than cumulative training	Enhance initial education and establish special compensatory training courses with certificates	"Back to school" incentives of various forms (e.g. subsidies, free time/sabbaticals with job return guarantee)
Outdated curricula	Revise and renew curricula frequently	Develop curricula on the basis of local knowledge
Unsuitable training sites and material	Invest in training sites and material (e.g. in the framework of World Bank poverty reduction strategies for low-income countries	
Bad training of trainers	Careful training of trainers; better cooperation between technical schools, universities, public and private sectors	
Lack of connection between training institutions and employers, and/or low level of private-sector involvement	Incentives for employers to train; establish certification at lower vocational levels (e.g. national vocational training certificates); create networks between employers and training institutions	
Difficulties of training in informal economy	Reach informal economy through promotion (e.g. skill campaigns)	Importance of general education, as a way to link formal schooling to informal work

Table 11.   (Cont.)

Problems	Various solutions sought by countries	Additional ideas
Overeducated and over-qualified unemployed	Find innovative ways to use their skills for, e.g. training others, job sharing	
Unequal access to training	Create incentives, financial or other (e.g. preferential placement support	
School-to-work transition	Reinforce cooperation between schools and private sector	
Financial bottlenecks	Use financial sources (e g. overseas development assistance, established funds, poverty reduction strategies); raise new, even small training levies if necessary and use them exclusively for training needs of firms and workers; give repayable grants to firms and/or workers	
Gender biases	Use potential of female labour force and end discrimination in training	

Public works / direct (public temporary) job creation

General:	*General:*	*General:*
Usually seen as make-work activities for marginal groups without effective re-employment chances; bad image, sometimes even leading to reduced employability of participants; uncertain link to (local) development strategies	Integrating public works schemes in (local) development strategies; integrating training in public works for better re-employment; enhancing image	Use it as one element of an activation strategy that copes with possible misuse of social benefits, while delivering useful public goods
Specific: Low labour market integration capacity	*Specific:* Anticipate end of measure by integrating training (e.g. for setting up on own account or takeover by private companies or in similar sector)	
End of measure equals return to poverty	Use measure to enhance living conditions and alleviate poverty (e.g. irrigation and road building for subsistence farmers)	
Establishment of permanent secondary labour markets	Enhance the transition of people to the regular labour market (framework of measure can be more permanent than participation of those passing through it)	

Table 11.   (Cont.)

Problems	Various solutions sought by countries	Additional ideas
Displacement of private sector	Build in "bridges" towards private sector activities (e.g. road and infrastructure maintenance)	
Stigmatization of participants	Engage in economically and socially useful activities; building in training	
Difficulty of enforcing work conditionality	Create efficient network of organizations (e.g. municipalities, NGOs) that can organize useful activities	
Gender bias	Create special programmes for women	

Employment subsidies

General:	*General:*	*General:*
Seldom used in developing countries; uncertain effects in informal sector; high dead-weight and substitution effect (especially when not targeted); problems of marginal tax rates after ending of subsidy	Use employment subsidies for specific targets, e.g. as compensation for low wages, or for initial periods of low productivity among specific target groups (e.g. unskilled young workers); in cyclical downturns; for reallocation of redundant workers	Combine programmes and make employment subsidies one of the instruments for bridge-building between employment policy programmes and regular jobs
Specific:	*Specific:*	
Timing of subsidy (in terms both of duration and of phasing in and out in relation to cycle)	Phase in at the onset of an upswing; create smooth transition when phasing out (e.g. degressive subsidy). Long-term subsidy to meet long-term needs	
		Specific:
Form of subsidy (tax rebate, negative income tax, wage premium)	Match to circumstances (e.g. when marginal tax rates are high, give tax rebate)	Consider the possibility of a negative income tax, which through registration can also contribute to formalizing informal work
Problematic for obsolete sectors	In such cases, use to compensate for wage differences between jobs lost and new jobs, or for restructuring purposes	
Informal economy	Use in-work benefits (wage premiums) for formalizing informal employment	Study tax rebates on the conditionality of job creation

Table 11.   (Cont.)

Problems	Various solutions sought by countries	Additional ideas

Self-employment, small enterprise creation

General:	*General:*	*General:*
Problem of targeting, and choices between maintaining and expanding existing SMEs and supporting the creation of new ones; activities of small firms and self-employed often at subsistence level with low productivity and low development potential	Give equal importance to helping existing firms at sensible growth thresholds and/or in temporary business slumps, and to supporting the creation of new ventures. Policy support for the latter should be well targeted to enable people to create enterprises, and should consist of providing access to subsidies and loans, as well as business advice	More networking between small and big firms integrated in local development frameworks; combination of policies (use of labour-intensive infrastructure investment programmes for establishing infrastructure serving the informal economy)
Specific:	*Specific:*	*Specific:*
Access to credit	Benefit capitalization for unemployed; loans and subsidies (also micro-finance); loan guarantees both for those setting up and those with the chance to stay in business but suffering temporary difficulties	Private and business sponsorship
Access to consultancy and training	One-stop shops for advice and interconnection between business community and creators	Use local knowledge in innovative ways
Low productivity	Advice on complementary activities, rationalization of processes and other means of enhancing productivity	Raise awareness of importance of organizing production processes
Informal sector	Incentives for registration: avoidance of high marginal tax rates for legalization; shortening transition periods; reducing bureaucratic hurdles	Introducing property rights; combination of salaried and self-employed work

Notes

[1] For a full account of the East Asian experience with ALMPs, see Betcherman et al. (2001).

[2] In countries where unemployment insurance and ALMP measures are mainly financed through taxes and levies on wages, the paradox emerges that in times of high unemployment the financial means to pay benefits (passive) crowd out the means for the active policies that are needed. This is less so when active policies are financed via the state budget.

[3] Argentina, Brazil, Chile, Costa Rica, Jamaica, Mexico and Peru. Figures on Latin America are calculated from Márquez (1999).

[4] See, for example, Devereux (2002) or Kanyenze et al. (2000).

[5] Programme participation rates = people participating in labour market programmes during a year as a percentage of the labour force.

[6] Figures are for 1995 and from Auer (2000).

[7] An excellent account of labour market experience in the East Asian countries after the crisis may be found in Betcherman and Islam (2001).

[8] For a full account of changes in PES, see also Thuy et al. (2001).

[9] Comprehensive information on the main characteristics of PES in OECD countries, as well as the new trends, is given in OECD (2000) and OECD (2007c).

[10] An exception was the former Yugoslavia, but because of the low unemployment level during socialism PES took on only limited functions.

[11] The information on transition countries is based on Nesporova (1999), pp. 64-66.

[12] The information on the East Asian countries in this and the following sections draws mainly on the recent work of Betcherman et al. (2001). Other sources are also indicated as appropriate.

[13] In a project of the Inter-American Development Bank a labour market information system was developed for Central American countries so that they can share and analyse data on a regional basis (Mazza, 2003).

[14] For specific country examples concerning PES and unemployment insurance see Marshall (1997, pp. 20-34; 2004, pp. 26-34)

[15] For a discussion of the applicability of unemployment insurance systems in Latin American countries refer to Mazza (2000).

[16] The following information is taken from Schulz and Klemmer (1998).

[17] Job rotation is mainly used in the Scandinavian countries and seems to have the highest take-up in the public sector. It was also implemented in employment legislation in Germany in January 2002.

[18] More information on the selectivity of training measures can be found in Schömann and O'Connell (2002) and in OECD (2003a), pp. 237-96.

[19] Unless indicated otherwise, information on East Asian countries draws on Betcherman et al. (2001).

[20] Information on the situation of training and education of rural youth in Asia and the Pacific, as well as examples from different countries, can be found in Asian Productivity Organization (2002a).

[21] Examples of strategies to tackle education and training needs of rural women are given in Asian Productivity Organization (2002b).

[22] A more detailed description of the Brazilian training body SENAI, created in 1942, and the model imitated by most Latin American countries, is offered by de Moura Castro et al. (2000), pp. 316-22.

[23] More information on innovative approaches to financing training can be found in Galhardi (2002).

[24] Information for this general introductory part is based on Nesporova (1999), pp. 55-58.

[25] OECD (2005b) provides an overview of the characteristics of specifie employment-conditional benefits in different OECD countries and discusses the role and effectiveness of in-work benefits.

[26] Levitsky and Hojmark Mikkelsen (2001) analyse the role of business development services in Latin America. Among other topics they deal with the role of the public sector in the establishment and operation of business development services.

FINANCING ALMPS

6

Competition in globalized economies renders demand for labour more volatile, which in turn might make workers more vulnerable (OECD, 2007a).[1] This in turn calls for more protection for workers; but this protection must be located outside firms, because firms subject to more intense competition, in both domestic and export markets, are usually less able to provide employment security through stable jobs. In simplistic terms, labour market security is the sum of employment protection in firms and social protection outside the firm. In the globalized, liberalized economies of today, the latter has to provide a larger share of worker protection than in the more closed and regulated economies of previous decades (Auer, 2007).

TYPES AND COSTS OF WORKER PROTECTION

What form, then, should worker protection outside the firm take? One element is of course the unemployment benefit system, the traditional provider of income security (and sometimes job reallocation in a different sector or location) for those out of work. Various forms of early retirement also play a role. However, there is a trend towards making labour market policies more active, and providing access to training or job creation schemes that may lead on to new jobs. What is needed is a credible and affordable security network, which offers security of both income and employability, and leads people into decent jobs. Meeting this need will involve labour market organizations responsible for designing, implementing and monitoring labour market policy, such as government departments and public employment services.

This analysis is linked to the concept of flexicurity, whose advocates see compensation for greater volatility in the formal labour sector being provided by more security through social protection. One of the criticisms made of flexicurity solutions is that they might encourage labour market flexibility, contributing to more volatile employment, but fail on security. At a time when jobs are increasingly precarious and budget restraints on social spending increasingly tight, such fears seem justified. However, a genuine system of labour market security would indeed ensure labour market flexibility (in the sense of allowing adjustment when justified on economic grounds) but would also protect workers' income and employability.

Active labour market policies (and indeed labour market policies in general) form a substantial part of any attempt to provide labour market security outside the employment relationship. However, they are costly. Denmark, certainly the ideal type of a country providing labour market security in a mobile labour market, spends up to 5 per cent of its GDP on this security (about 1.5-1.8 per cent on ALMPs). Similar spending patterns are found only in the Netherlands and Sweden. This level of spending, of course, could not easily be matched by other countries, and especially not by low-income countries.

The European Commission has come up with some interesting estimates of what other EU countries would have to spend on LMPs and ALMPs to match the outlay of the three highest-spending countries. On average, the 22 EU countries included in the calculations would have to spend around 4 per cent of GDP more on labour market policies (about 2.5 per cent on PLMPs and 1.5 per cent on ALMPs) to equal the level of spending per unemployed person found in Denmark, Sweden and the Netherlands. For some of the new Member States, such as Slovakia, where unemployment is high and spending on labour market policies low, this would mean allocating an additional 12 per cent of GDP to this area, which is next to impossible. However, while increases of this magnitude would be out of the question, more spending on LMPs, and in particular on ALMPs, is on the agenda, and may be supported in its initial phase through the EU's structural funds.

For developing countries, finding a source of funds for spending on a labour market security network is more difficult. All available options will need to be considered, from social contributions collected through payroll taxes to revenues from general taxation (on, for example, primary goods exports or consumption), international aid and remittances.

Although the costs of an adequate labour market security system are substantial, the crude estimates referred to above do not take into account the positive impact of LMPs, including ALMPs, on the labour market and the economy. This positive impact is clearly apparent in the countries that spend most on these programmes, which show a very good labour market record that does not jeopardize economic efficiency but contributes to social and economic equity, providing evidence of the benefits to be reaped from such an active policy stance. The same picture emerges from the OECD's *Employment Outlook 2006*, which puts the Anglo-Saxon countries ("mainly English speaking countries"), which are usually low spenders on LMPs, on a par with the Nordic countries ("mainly North European countries") in terms of economic and labour market performance, but also shows that the latter do much better in equity terms, achieving low levels of poverty and relatively equal income distribution.

HOW SHOULD LABOUR MARKET POLICY BE FINANCED?

In the developed countries there is a debate on whether it is better to finance labour market policy through the general budget or through specific wage-based social security contributions. This debate reflects the division between tax-based, means-tested and universal coverage systems (often referred to as Beveridge systems), and contribution-based systems, which are linked to former earnings and usually not universal (referred to as Bismarckian systems).[2] There are arguments for and against both these modes of financing. Schmid, Reissert and Bruche (1992) argue that ALMPs should be financed out of the general budget, because otherwise there is a tendency for active measures to be eclipsed by passive measures in times of rising unemployment, when revenue from contributions will remain stable or shrink while expenditure on unemployment benefits will rise. As both active and passive policies are paid for out of the same fund, but unemployment benefits (as an insurance right) take precedence over ALMPs (which are usually discretionary), the former will crowd out the latter. This, Schmid et al. contend, is what has happened in Germany: an outcome that could have been avoided, they argue, if active policies had been financed out of the general budget, and only passive policies out of contributions, as for example is the case in Sweden. Of course, making participation in ALMPs a right and an obligation, as is the case in Denmark, would also do the trick.

Another argument suggests that high non-wage labour costs (such as those exacted by payroll taxes to fund LMPs) have a negative effect on employment by giving rise to a high "tax wedge", that is, the difference between gross and net wages. A high wedge, it is argued, is detrimental to employment for both demand- and supply-side reasons, especially for workers at the lower end of the pay scale. Employers are deterred from hiring because of high labour costs, and the unemployed would remain longer on benefits – assuming such benefits are available – through reluctance to take on low-paid work. It is no coincidence that there are many labour market policies that tackle the wedge, for example by exempting young people from social contributions to make them cheaper to employ, while maintaining their income. This in turn has led to a preference for funding LMPs out of the general tax system, and to a shift in the source of funding from social contributions to other forms of taxation, such as value added tax, as recently happened in Germany.

While there is less support today than formerly for extending the financing of social security through contributions, in many OECD countries the existing social security systems, especially unemployment insurance systems, are more often contribution-based than tax-based. The OECD reckons that social contributions and other earmarked revenues are the main funding source for social security in general, providing about 60 per cent of total finance (OECD, 2007a).[3] The ILO's Employment Promotion and Protection against Unemployment Convention, 1988, foresees countries choosing freely between the two modes of financing.[4]

In developing countries, contributions from both employers and workers would be indispensable as a basis for introducing any such system. Such information as is available on unemployment systems in developing countries indicates this is indeed the case. As a consequence, unemployment benefit systems are essentially limited to the formal sector.

There is also debate on how best to divide the burden of contributions between employers and workers. Various models exist, from wholly employer-financed systems to more strongly worker-based systems: in France, employers provide 63 per cent of contributions, workers 37 per cent, while in Germany workers and employers contribute 50 per cent each. However, this applies only to funding for unemployment insurance. In general, the trend in funding for non-insurance, solidarity-based assistance systems for those out of work, and especially for ALMPs, is towards tax-based systems – as for example in the recent German labour market reforms, which established means-tested basic revenue for those who are unemployed or no longer eligible for insurance benefits.

CHOOSING AN APPROPRIATE FUNDING SYSTEM

To conclude this brief review of the funding options for ALMPs, and to offer some food for thought to countries considering them, it is worth stressing the need for, and benefits of, such policies. There are many ways to finance passive and active labour market policies, but irrespective of which path they choose, countries would be well advised to accept the principle of the need for more protection in the face of globalization, and to start laying the foundations for labour market policies if they are interested in providing labour market security for their workers. In addition, as noted by the OECD and others, social protection is itself a productive factor and, "if well designed, will have positive productivity effects associated with its funding" (OECD, 2007a, p. 159).

The financing system chosen should be well assessed and tailored to the individual country's needs. The available options comprise a range of variants on the two main types: those based on social contributions (which may be kept to a minimum level to avoid "tax wedges", at least in the formal sector) and those based on taxes (income, company and consumption taxes, and combinations thereof).

As for the employment effects of different forms of financing LMPs, it may be true that "for a given tax revenue a partial shift from social contributions to income or consumption taxes may have favourable employment effects" (OECD, 2007a, p. 160) in developed countries. For developing countries the choice of the "right" financing system is trickier. While keeping the employment effect in mind, it is necessary also to balance the tax base carefully in order not to punish job creation and encourage the informal sector. Consumption taxes are one way to raise revenue for public spending on labour market security, but rising prices exacerbate poverty.

To help developing countries wishing to establish a system of worker protection, some seed money in the form of donor contributions could also be envisaged. These contributions might be collected into a "global trust fund" as proposed by the ILO (2007). Even proceeds of international taxes, whenever available (for example, Tobin taxes on financial transactions) could be used.

The division between centralized and decentralized funding also needs to be carefully assessed. While local administrations (at, say region or county level) usually know local needs better than central government administrations, decentralized funding carries a risk of poor administration, corruption and nepotism. All decentralized systems, whether funded centrally or locally, must include provisions for sound monitoring and feedback to ensure efficient fund administration (Auer and Kruppe, 1996).

Notes

[1] Many of the arguments in this chapter are taken from a recent report for the ILO: M. Pointecker, *Financing active labour market policies* (Geneva, ILO, forthcoming)

[2] Beveridge was a British economist and social reformer who proposed this system in a report of 1942. Bismarck was the German empire's prime minister in the late nineteenth century, under whom social security was introduced and extended.

[3] Countries which finance dominantly through contributions are France, Belgium, most Central and Eastern European countries, and also the Republic of Korea. General taxation is usual in Denmark, Australia, Canada and the United Kingdom.

[4] The convention has been ratified by only seven countries.

EVALUATION OF ALMPS

7

In the light of the ongoing controversy concerning the economic case for and the effectiveness of ALMPs, the monitoring and evaluation of these programmes is highly significant in many respects. First, the credibility of ALMP measures will very much depend on how successful they are in achieving the policy goals they were designed to meet. Second, by the same token, the justification of implementing ALMPs is contingent upon how efficiently the limited funds for employment promotion have been spent in pursuing these policy objectives (opportunity costs). Third, regular monitoring and evaluation of ALMPs offer invaluable feedback for modifying and adjusting these policies to achieve better results. Increased impact of these policies can only be accomplished by steady improvement of their design and implementation, informed by rigorous evaluation research.

DIFFERENT MODELS FOR EVALUATION

Thorough ALMP programme evaluation has been neglected for a long time. But now – with advanced statistical techniques at hand and a range of best-practice evaluation examples – policy-makers as well as scientists are increasingly interested in evaluation results to enable them to adapt and improve programme design. The choice of evaluation technique and methodology becomes crucial for reaching the right conclusions about the effectiveness of alternative labour market measures. The *International handbook of labour market policy and evaluation* (Schmid et al., 1996, pp. 2-6) usefully distinguishes between target-oriented and programme-oriented policy evaluation, and highlights the significance of considering policy formation and implementation processes while evaluating the success of any programme. The approach offered is target-oriented evaluation, which stresses not only the importance of measuring the impact of policies in terms of reaching their targets, but also the crucial role played by "the incentives created by the interaction of different policy interventions and the cumulative impact of policy regimes on the disposition and observable behaviour of the relevant actors in the target area". Target-oriented evaluation is thus a "bottom-up" approach, whereby the effects of policies are viewed from the perspective of the relevant agents and the process of policy formation and implementation is not considered as a black box. While programme-oriented evaluation assesses the impact of one programme designated for a specific target, target-oriented evaluation assesses the impact of various programmes with a view to reaching a specific target, such as increased employment options for the hard-to-place or facilitation of school-to-work transition, and allows for the comparison of different programmes designed for reaching a common target.

As Meager and Evans (1998) point out, however, there are very few evaluation studies that adopt such a perspective. In general, evaluation techniques concerning the impact of labour market programmes are basically divided into three groups: experimental, quasi-experimental and non-experimental. Experimental impact evaluation refers to those studies that select both treatment and control groups prior to the commencement of the labour market programme. Treatment groups are those benefiting from the programme, while control groups are those that are not receiving assistance through the specific programme under evaluation. Experimental evaluations are costly and time-consuming, and are mainly used in North America and to a much lesser degree in Europe.[1]

There are a number of problems associated with experimental evaluation methods: first of all, it can be unethical to deny services provided by a programme to eligible persons; cooperation from the administrators of the programme is essential to evaluation success; and there is the risk that administrators and participants will behave differently during the experiment from how they would under normal circumstances. Another problem that arises especially in European countries is the fact that experiments usually focus on the impact of a specific programme without taking into account the interactions of active programmes or the functioning of various ALMPs as an integrated system of measures (Björklund and Regnér, 1996, pp. 112-13). Quasi-experimental evaluation studies choose treatment and control groups after the policy intervention, by using survey data on participants and data on the unemployed with comparable characteristics who did not participate in the ALMP measure (for example, from PES data or labour force survey data). Recent evaluation also uses longitudinal data that follow individuals over a number of years and can thus assess the impact of specific active interventions on, for example, post-participation earnings or job tenure. In recent years, quasi-experimental evaluation designs have become standard in most OECD countries.

Non-experimental evaluation techniques, on the other hand, do not use control groups in their approach and rely merely on statistics or other relevant information compiled by programme administrators, which render such studies less informative. Since information on what might have happened in the absence of the specific programme is missing from these studies, they cannot determine whether the participants of the programme benefit from it. However, non-experimental evaluation studies offer some insight on deadweight losses, substitution and displacement effects. They can also help to determine if target groups were reached by a specific measure. In developing countries hampered by a lack of more advanced data collection and a scarcity of funding for evaluation measures, non-experimental evaluation studies often constitute the only available option.

EVALUATION RESULTS

LMP evaluation research has indeed shown that not all active measures are efficient in reaching their target groups; not all enhance the chances of participants to access jobs after participation; and not all are cost-effective means to reach their set goals. LMP evaluation has evolved from being relatively simple to a very complex tool for policy-makers. The most advanced evaluation techniques operate with carefully selected control groups and aim at comparing the effectiveness of different programmes in reaching a common target. Evaluation research gives useful information to policy-makers, but it does not appear that evaluation results are always followed by appropriate policy action. This is in part because results are sometimes contradictory or ambiguous.

The outcomes of a series of evaluation studies have been studied from four recent sources, namely Meager and Evans (1998, pp. 29-57), Betcherman et al. (2001, pp. 314-15), Martin and Grubb (2001, p. 24) and Betcherman et al. (2004, pp. 18-55). These are here combined into one table, thus presenting a comprehensive picture of the available evidence on ALMP evaluation (table 12). Owing to the scarcity of evaluation studies on developing countries, the evidence presented focuses mainly on evaluation results of ALMP measures in OECD countries.

These evaluation overview studies show that the effects of programmes on employment and wages are usually small and positive, but not in all cases. These results have to do with several perverse effects such as deadweight (the same result would have been achieved in the absence of a programme), substitution (subsidized persons may displace non-subsidized persons), displacement (subsidized activities may displace other activities in the economy) and creaming (only the most employable among the unemployed obtain access to jobs through policy intervention). As can be seen from table 12, evaluation studies reveal that in general ALMPs seem to be rather effective for women and labour market re-entrants, but seldom for young people. Women's (and especially women re-entrants') chances of integration success through ALMPs can be strengthened by offering additional childcare services or contributions to childcare costs. Wage subsidies to employers or employees seem to serve especially the needs of the long-term unemployed, while self-employment schemes and micro-enterprise development programmes often show more

Table 12. Evaluation results for ALMPs

Programme	Source	Appear to help	Comments
Job-search assistance and employment services (26 evaluations)	D&T B&O&D	Unemployed adults when economic conditions are improving; women may benefit more; youth	Relatively more cost-effective than other labour market interventions (such as training) due to low intervention costs. Possible deadweight losses if not effectively targeted. Quite successful in developed and transition countries, but less successful in selected developing countries
Counselling/advice, job-search assistance/training, etc. (13 evaluations)	M&E	Unemployed adults, but especially the long-term unemployed	Enhanced labour market and earning effects, especially for target groups. More cost-effective. Only one evaluation showed negative effects for participants compared to control group
Job-search assistance (job clubs, individual counselling, etc.)	M&G	Most unemployed, but in particular, women and single parents	Must be combined with increased monitoring of the job-search behaviour of the unemployed and enforcement of work tests
Of which: re-employment bonuses		Most adult unemployed	Requires careful monitoring and controls on both recipients and their former employers
Training for long-term unemployed (28 evaluations)	D&T	Women and other disadvantaged groups	No more effective than job-search assistance in increasing re-employment probabilities and post-intervention earnings; two to four times more costly
Formal classroom training	M&G	Women re-entrants. Does not appear to help prime-age men and older workers with low initial education	Important that courses have strong labour market relevance, or signal "high" quality to employers. Should lead to a qualification that is recognized and valued by employers. Keep programmes relatively small in scale
On-the-job training	M&G	Women re-entrants; single mothers	Must directly meet labour market needs. Hence, need to establish strong links with local employers, but this increases the risk of displacement
Retraining workers displaced in mass lay-offs (12 evaluations)	D&T	Little positive impact; positive results mainly when economy is improving	No more effective than job-search assistance and significantly more expensive. Rate of return usually negative

Table 12.   (Cont.)

Programme	Source	Appear to help	Comments
Training for youth (7 evaluations)	D&T	No positive impact	Employment and earning prospects not improved. Negative real rate of return to these programmes when costs are taken into account. Additional evaluation shows positive employment impact in developing countries
(12 additional evaluations)	B&O&D	Positive impact in developing countries	
Training (vocational skills) (36 evaluations)	M&E	Disadvantaged groups; especially prime-aged women	Results patchy, but positive effects on employment and earnings are as commonplace as no or negative effect. Higher positive impact when training involves placement with a private sector employer. Appears less effective than other active measures, especially direct job creation, where compared. Evidence of creaming, deadweight and substitution effects
Work-sharing/reducing labour supply (1 evaluation)	M&E		Participants less likely to enter permanent or temporary employment than non-participants or than those benefiting from other active measures (training, public works, etc.)
Employment and wage subsidies (45 evaluations)	D&T	Long-term unemployed	Benefits to treatment group not significant compared with control group. Sometimes used by firms as a permanent subsidy programme. High deadweight and substitution effects
Subsidies to employment	M&G	Long-term unemployed; women re-entrants	Require careful targeting and adequate controls to maximize net employment gains, but there is a trade-off with employer take-up
Of which: aid to unemployed starting enterprises		Men (below 40, relatively better educated)	Only works for a small subset of the unemployed
Subsidies for employers (16 evaluations)	M&E	Disadvantaged groups such as long-term unemployed, unskilled youth, welfare recipients, disabled or women out of employment for a long time	Positive impact, but usually with high deadweight and substitution effects, implying lower net impact. Only one case of no positive impact on employment
Subsidized short-term placements with employers (1 evaluation)	M&E		Participants less likely to enter permanent or temporary employment than non-participants or those benefiting from other active measures, especially replacement schemes

Table 12. (Cont.)

Programme	Source	Appear to help	Comments
Subsidies to individuals (1 evaluation)	M&E	Long-term unemployed	Subsidies to start low-paid jobs. High deadweight, but also high percentage still in jobs after end of subsidy
In-work benefits (2 evaluations)	B&O&D	Welfare recipients	Substantial employment and earning effect
Public works programmes (28 evaluations)	D&T B&O&D	Severely disadvantaged groups and unemployed in general	Long-term unemployment prospects not helped. Programme participants less likely to be hired for permanent jobs than control group and less likely to earn the same wage. Not cost-effective if objective is to get people into gainful employment. Good as safety net, low performance as labour market integration tool
Direct job creation	M&G	Does not appear to help most adult and youth unemployed	Typically provides few long-term benefits and principle of additionality usually implies low marginal-product jobs
Direct employment: Traditional job creation and intermediate labour market schemes (23 evaluations)	M&E	Unqualified unemployed and youth	Positive effects on subsequent employment and income levels. More short-term employment advantages than long-term, perhaps due to employers' negative views about participation in such programmes. Those with no qualifications increased their chances of staying in employment more than those with some skills. In some cases, high displacement, deadweight and substitution effects
Micro-enterprise development programmes (15 evaluations, 6 new added by B&O&D)	D&T B&O&D	Relatively senior and more educated groups No indication on target group	Very low take-up rate among unemployed. Significant failure rate of small businesses. High deadweight and displacement effects. High costs — cost-benefit analyses rarely conducted, but sometimes show higher costs than for control group. In some cases better firm survival, especially in transition countries
Self-employment schemes (9 evaluations)	M&E	Better-qualified adults	Positive effects in terms of aggregate employment in the majority of cases. Sometimes significant indirect job-creation effects. Deadweight and displacement effects occasionally high

Table 12. (Cont.)

Programme	Source	Appear to help	Comments
Comparative evaluations across schemes (4 evaluations)	M&E	Full range of Irish ALMP measures	• Market-oriented schemes (specific rather than general skills-training; indirect job-creation via subsidies rather than direct job-creation) had highest impact in terms of short- and medium-term employment effects and post-programme earnings • Individual characteristics, notably educational qualifications and previous labour market experience, are also important
		Three schemes in the United Kingdom: work placements (Work Trials); job-search assistance (Job Clubs); and improved job matching (Job-Interview Guarantee)	• All three programmes have substantial short-term employment impacts, net of deadweight • Work Trials has biggest short-term effect • Job Clubs and improved job matching have significant effects for women and unqualified men • No significant wage impact
		Range of employment measures in eastern Germany	Traditional measures of public-sponsored training are less effective in terms of employment effects than are firm-sponsored training measures, regardless whether they are on or off the job
		42 recent ALMP measures in the United Kingdom	• Training measures have highest unit costs, not compensated by short term placement effects • Job-search measures have lowest unit costs, but smaller than average net employment effect • Employer subsidies have low take-up and high deadweight, resulting in high net costs per job • In-work benefits have some impact on unemployment trap, but do not provide route to higher-paid employment • Subsidies to individuals in finding/taking work have lowest cost per job
Special youth measures (training, employment subsidies, direct job-creation measures)	M&G	Do not appear to help disadvantaged youth	Effective programmes need to combine an appropriate and integrated mix of education, occupational skills, work-based learning and supportive services to young people and their families Early and sustained interventions are likely to be most effective. Need to deal with inappropriate attitudes to work on the part of youth. Adult mentors can help

Source: Dar and Tzannatos (D&T), 1999; reported in Betcherman et al. (2001, pp. 314-315); Martin and Grubb (M&G), 1998; Meager and Evans (M&E), 1998; Betcherman, Olivas and Dar (B&O&D), 2004.

success among better-qualified individuals and especially men. All in all, as job-search assistance is the most cost-effective measure, it should be intensively used over all phases of unemployment.

When it comes to designing other ALMP measures, it is important to reserve time for job-search activities in order not to prolong unemployment accidentally through active measures – recently some active programmes (e.g. the Community Works Programme in New Zealand) have made use of this lesson. Evaluation results for training measures are very mixed. Generally, content and skills that are taught should closely match the demand on the labour market; training should be certified; and it should take place in close cooperation with private sector employers. Public works programmes prove to be helpful only for severely disadvantaged groups who have hardly any chance of finding employment in the regular labour market. They tend also to develop in secondary labour markets with low chances of transition to regular jobs. In addition, public works in OECD countries are usually comparatively costly. However, as the examples in Chapter 5 showed, in developing countries public works, especially in the field of construction, can have important multiplier effects. Furthermore, in the absence of passive welfare benefits they contribute to keeping the poorest segments of society above subsistence level. Usually, programmes that incorporate a range of different services seem to be more effective.[2]

Some of the evaluation studies clearly reveal the positive impact of ALMPs in terms of reducing unemployment. In France, for example, it is estimated that community work has a high impact on the reduction of unemployment and prevents new unemployment spells at a rate of 60 to 70 per cent on average for each subsidized public works job (DARES, 1996). In Germany, ALMPs contributed substantially to the reduction of open unemployment, especially during reunification. Likewise, ALMPs lowered the unemployment rate in Argentina by 0.8 percentage points in 1999, 0.6 in 2000 and 0.7 in 2001. In Chile, the effects were even higher (1.0, 0.7 and 1.5 percentage points, respectively).[3] In addition, opportunity cost analyses revealed that ALMPs for the unemployed have a low net cost for public budgets because of their unemployment prevention effects. A recent evaluation overview found that only around 60 per cent of all screened evaluation reports showed positive post-participation employment effects (Betcherman et al., 2004). Many evaluation studies are also cautious in terms of longer-term labour market integration of programme participants.

Evaluation studies usually measure only the economic effects of ALMPs, which clearly also have social goals. Even the measurement of the economic effects seems to be too narrow, as only the employment effect (has the person been integrated into the labour market?) and the wage effect (have wages increased after participation?) are typically measured. The net value of a programme cannot be assessed, however, without taking into account the positive multiplier effects of spending on programmes or its endogenous growth effects. Many studies in the 1970s and 1980s indeed showed high multiplier effects for some of the measures, especially for public works programmes.[4]

One clearly must go back to these and reinvent evaluation techniques that take into account the positive spill-over effects of, for example, infrastructure creation through public works or the setting up of new enterprises through micro-credit programmes, as well as the social effects of these measures.

Yet the effects of ALMPs are not limited to those mentioned above, as there are also general arguments in favour of ALMPs, for example, with regard to decent work. Recent, as yet unpublished, ILO work shows that expenditure on ALMPs correlates positively with the perception of employment security and with job quality, suggesting that those policies have a positive impact on decent work by providing a safety net in case of job loss. Positively perceived employment security also has beneficial impacts on the macro economy via consumption behaviour (see box).

Consumption smoothing through LMP expenditure

One aspect of LMP expenditure has received little attention in the literature on labour market policies, namely the macroeconomic demand and stability benefits of such policies. Labour market expenditure, be it active or passive, if spent efficiently, can provide the basis for ensuring demand stability and/or growth and hence prevent the adverse impacts of economic downturns from snowballing. The process can best be exemplified by considering the local economic effects of mass dismissal. If such a social shock to the local economy is not cushioned by either passive policies such as unemployment insurance or active policies such as public works and self-employment promotion, or indeed both, the decrease in consumption demand of laid-off workers, as well as the fall in consumption of other members of the local community due to increased job insecurity, will potentially lead to an economic shock to the system which is over and above the initial shock The snowball effect of such a reduction in local consumption would in turn adversely affect the livelihood of those in the local community. Aggregation of such effects over the entire economy could not only exacerbate the negative outcomes of an economic recession, but also constitute a serious demand constraint along with its associated multiplier effects and render economic recovery difficult. However, a well-developed social protection system with effective labour market institutions capable of efficiently using active and passive policies may help distribute the burden of lay-offs more equitably among different economic agents, and thus mitigate the adverse consequences of economic slumps.

Indeed, according to a study by Wolter (1998) on the costs of job insecurity in Switzerland during the economic recession in the 1990s, increased job insecurity adversely affected consumer spending in the country, aggravating the negative effects of the economic downturn via the multiplier. Based on scenario simulations, the author estimates that as a result of the consumption forgone due to diminished job security, GDP growth rates were half of what they would have been. Likewise, Chimerine et al. (1999) estimate that in the United States the unemployment insurance programme mitigated the loss in real GDP by approximately 15 per cent during the five recessions that occurred between 1969 and the early 1990s. The programme exhibited a substantial and significant countercyclical effect on changes in real GDP

---

over the three decades, resulting in an average peak savings of 131,000 jobs. Based on a household-level analysis of the effect of unemployment insurance on consumption, Gruber (1997), on the other hand, finds that in the absence of unemployment insurance, becoming unemployed would be associated with a fall in consumption of 22 per cent, compared with the 6.8 per cent drop for unemployment insurance recipients in the United States. Finally, Orszag (2001) calculates that, in comparison with other stimulus measures, such as income tax cuts, the American unemployment insurance system is at least eight times as effective as the tax system as a whole in offsetting the impact of a recession.

In summary, both theory and evidence implicate that the scope for LMPs to contribute to the alleviation of labour market outcomes is not only limited to social cushioning but also involves wider economic consequences. In other words, the case for LMPs is both social and economic. At the macroeconomic level, improved social protection via active and passive policies delivered by effective labour market institutions can become an indispensable part of the basis for a virtuous circle, whereby adverse employment outcomes of economic policies can be mitigated and increased productivity levels associated with better social protection can be attained (see forthcoming work of Auer et al. for microeconomic evidence on productivity and job tenure).

Despite such evident theoretical arguments and supporting empirical findings, to our knowledge there has been no systematic research on the historical trends and interactions between LMP expenditure and aggregate consumption. Changes in LMP expenditure are associated with variations in household final consumption expenditure (HFCE), as shown by the graphs below on Germany, Spain and Sweden. They plot the development of expenditure on passive and active labour market policies, as well as of the HFCE as a percentage of GDP between 1985 and 2001. It can be seen that in most cases consumption spending varies positively with expenditure on active and especially passive measures — a consumption smoothing function of LMPs can thus be deduced. Work on this issue is still very preliminary and further research is called for in order to establish robust tests for the correlation between consumption and LMP expenditure.

Consumption and LMP expenditure as % of GDP in Germany: 1985-2001

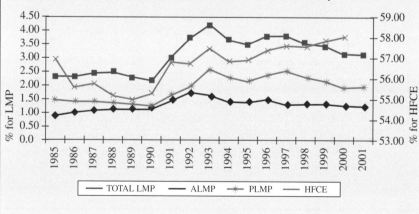

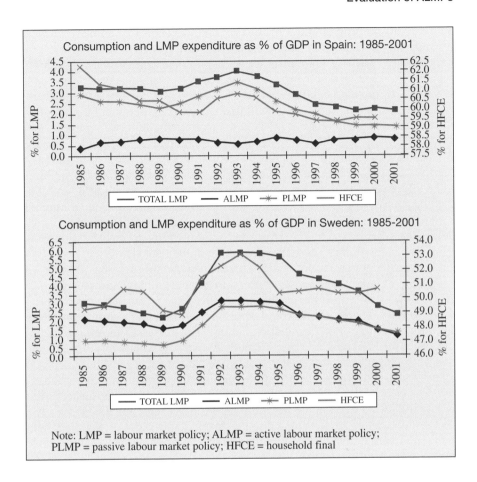

Note: LMP = labour market policy; ALMP = active labour market policy;
PLMP = passive labour market policy; HFCE = household final

Although evaluation research cannot yet account for all these different aspects of ALMPs, some lessons for improved policy design can still be drawn. Some of the results of existing evaluation studies can be summarized as follows. In general, carefully targeted measures achieve better results than broad measures applying to everyone or larger groups. However, close targeting that avoids deadweight is inversely related to take-up: targeted programmes are usually small and hence do not reach many unemployed. Measures that are closer to real-life experience (real work situations) achieve better results than measures that are remote from regular labour market activities. Thus it seems important to have private sector participation in the programmes. This is particularly true for training but also for public works schemes, which have to avoid being pure "make-work" schemes, but contribute to real value added. One way of doing so would be to integrate public works programmes into labour-intensive investment strategies.[5]

Evaluation research has also looked at delivery and programme administration. A summary of results indicates that decentralization seems to yield better results for programme delivery. However, decentralized delivery systems require a monitoring system that compares the results of the decentralized units (e.g. public or private employment services or training centres) and yields information for programme delivery divergence, thereby enabling corrective action. If targets, formulated centrally, focus too strongly on cost-effectiveness, the danger exists that administrators will make use of creaming and thus neglect the harder-to-place in order to fulfil these targets. Possibilities to prevent such strategies are the careful setting of targets for the inclusion of groups that are discriminated against or the higher valuation of achievements to include the hard-to-place in ALMPs in the overall assessment. Decentralization, in order to be effective, requires a centralized policy-setting and monitoring unit. On the other hand, evaluation literature finds that one-stop shops, integrating all services provided to jobseekers, are preferable to having dispersed agencies delivering such services. Therefore, the trend towards decentralization goes hand-in-hand with increased integration of employment services.

Given the importance of ALMPs for the new security frameworks that we call "labour market security" as opposed to job and employment security (see Auer, 2007) it is indeed important that these policies work in terms of delivering security. Therefore we would echo the European Commission in calling for the cultivation of an "evaluation culture" (European Commission, 2006) that checks the effectiveness of these policies more systematically and uses the results to make them work better. This systematic evaluation should apply to all efforts to activate labour markets, from intensive job search to an obligation to work (workfare), for results are often unclear and policy-makers need clarity if they are to continue fruitfully on this track (OECD, 2007a).

These debates are not limited to the developed world. For example, both India and China have embarked on large ALMP programmes; examples include the employment guarantee programme in India and the new effort of the Chinese government to create a unified rural-urban labour market, again with the help of active (and passive) policies. These large-scale programmes must be closely monitored and evaluated, and some of their design features might change when the results of evaluation are available.

Notes

[1] Some examples of experimental programme evaluation in North America and Europe are given in Björklund and Regnér (1996) and in Schmid et al. (1996), pp. 89-114.

[2] More detailed information on evaluation results for different programme types and for country-specific ALMP programmes is given in Fay (1996).

[3] These figures might overestimate the effects of active programmes on the unemployment rate, since the programmes may have attracted persons who had not been active in the labour market, as also admitted by the ILO's *2001 Labour Overview*, p. 18.

[4] See e.g. Spitznagel (1975).

[5] See e.g. Devereux (2002) or Lyby (2001).

NEW TRENDS IN ALMPS

8

An important and far-reaching new trend in LMPs is **activation**.[1] The EU's European Employment Strategy of 1997, now integrated in the larger EU Lisbon Strategy that aims at making the EU the most competitive and inclusive knowledge economy in the world by 2010, promotes active over passive policies as a means both to raise employment rates and to diminish the financial burden on the social welfare system. Accordingly, ALMPs play an important role in several of the 24 integrated economic and employment guidelines that the EU Commission has issued for the period 2005-08. Guideline 19 of the EES calls for active, preventive and individualized labour market measures including early identification of needs, job search assistance, guidance and training, as well as the provision of necessary social services to support the inclusion of those furthest from the labour market (European Council, 2005). Activation entails a new balance between the rights and duties of the unemployed, by introducing conditionality. In many Member States, job search, employment take-up and participation in active measures are increasingly enforced. After a defined period (usually up to six months for young people and up to 12 months for adults) during which the unemployed can receive benefits almost unconditionally except for the job search requirement (the frequency of obligatory reporting on job search activities varies widely between countries), the activation period (more intensive job search, training or temporary public work schemes) sets in.

A further form of activation that is increasingly used in OECD countries is **in-work benefits**, which set incentives to take up employment in low-paid jobs by offering income supplements. Activation has been an important element of the labour market recovery in some countries and is linked to the concept of **transitional labour markets**, which aim at promoting increased mobility by achieving security through passive and especially active LMPs.[2] Such protected mobility – or "flexicurity" – enables a strategy for management of change that targets flows rather than stocks on the labour market. Among institutions and policies allowing for protected mobility, ALMPs are an important instrument and thus can enhance the structural adjustment capacity of labour markets.

Within the policies around the nexus of labour market flexibility and security, ALMPs have an important role both as instruments for lifelong learning and as general policies for ensuring "protected mobility" in transitions between jobs, between jobs and unemployment, and from school to work and from work to retirement. Indeed, as shown at the beginning of this book, countries with open trading regimes that have successfully reformed their labour markets and show high levels of adaptability and security have used ALMPs in the process. Accordingly, among the common principles on flexicurity adopted by the European Council of Ministers at the end of 2007 in Lisbon, ALMPs figure prominently. Indeed, alongside passive policies and social protection policies, active policies play a crucial role in providing the new security framework in the more open and volatile labour markets of globalized economies. Therefore, one cannot be complacent about these policies: they have to be made fit for the task and must deliver the security element of promised "flexicurity" solutions without jeopardizing the capacity of firms to adapt. As was shown in the preceding chapter, evaluation gives hints on how to make such policies better and on which policies to use for which purposes. "What works for whom?" should therefore be an important question asked by labour market policy-makers and implementation agents.

To address this question of what works for whom, **profiling techniques and individual job action plans** have been developed to assess the unemployed person's employability situation on the labour market and to provide tailor-made programmes for dealing with an individual's or group's "binding constraints" in order to guarantee access to jobs. Such binding constraints on the supply side of the labour market include insufficient information on available jobs, insufficient job search capacities, inadequate education and training, and/or mobility barriers (e.g. access to housing). Other constraints (mainly in developed countries) may be inadequate wages or demeaning jobs that, despite being available, are not filled. In this case, profiling can be used to determine the needs of an individual searching for jobs. Profiling techniques and individual job action plans have increasingly been used in the EU Member States, including the transition economies. Profiling techniques are used in a number of countries as a diagnostic tool to enable (individualized) measures to be better targeted and thereby more effective in finding work for the unemployed.[3] Usually, demographic characteristics, skills, experiences and social situation are taken into account. In order to fix the rights and duties of the unemployed, as well as outlining an individually adapted active strategy for finding re-employment, individual action plans are used in almost all OECD countries (OECD, 2007c, pp. 226-28), but are not always required in the initial stage of unemployment. While the danger of "workfare" is present in such strategies, they often also establish a right to participation in ALMPs or access to other supporting measures.

However, working on the supply side alone will not be enough. Labour market policies, both active and passive, have to be accompanied by adequate growth policies, to create an adequate number of jobs to which people can be transferred. These include in particular "active" employment policies that are not developed further in this volume, such as adequate macroeconomic policies (e.g. creating the conditions for labour-intensive job growth through monetary and fiscal policies) and a regulatory environment that supports job creation.

In the narrower framework of active labour market policies, supply-side measures such as training need to be complemented by demand-enhancing ALMPs such as temporary job creation programmes, wage subsidies and enterprise creation schemes . One measure, frequently applied by developed countries, that supports activation strategies is **in-work benefits**, which set incentives to take up employment in low-paid jobs by offering income supplements.

Many countries across the world have shifted or are shifting from largely state-run and/or planned economies towards more market-oriented economies that are to a lesser degree subject to government intervention in the labour market. Therefore, new – or at least more efficient – **labour market intermediation** is required to manage the various changes in the labour market and to provide for adequate matching processes, income and employability through efficient delivery of passive – and especially active – LMPs.

Another new and related development which can be observed in many regions is **socially sensitive enterprise restructuring**. The processes and policies used to accompany workers made redundant because of company restructuring are a very important element of economic transitions. Their objective is to allow for outplacement through ALMPs such as training and retraining, enterprise creation or wage subsidies. If maintaining workers is a viable option, so-called **employment and competitiveness pacts** are concluded in some countries: these usually swap employment maintenance for wage moderation or working time reductions. The dramatic consequences of downsizing for families and whole regions make the issue a priority for employment policies.

All the above points to the need for countries to have permanent labour market institutions for the management of change that fulfil the double objective of allowing for flexibility so that change can occur and providing security in change. LMPs for the management of change that especially help the most vulnerable labour market groups must evolve into permanent instruments for the more open and flowing labour markets that accompany globalization.

The OECD countries most open to globalization are also the ones that have the densest network of labour market institutions to protect their workers against the adverse effects of globalization (Agell, 1999, p. 453). If permanent institutions such as an unemployment insurance system complemented by a labour exchange and ALMPs exist, changes in the labour market will be facilitated as workers enjoy more security. These institutions accompanying change also have a bearing on decent work. While it holds true that decent and productive work requires an employment relationship of some length, decent jobs are also affected by change (Auer and Cazes, 2003), and it is important that those losing jobs can rely on an income and on secure employability.

Notes

[1] Examples of policy initiatives in several OECD countries in activating the unemployed are given by Gilbert and Van Voorhis (2001). A very good overview of activation trends in OECD countries is given in OECD (2007c), pp. 272-42.

[2] More information on this concept and its theoretical foundation, as well as examples of its use, are given in Schmid and Gazier (2002).

[3] For an overview of which countries use profiling techniques, see OECD (2007c, p. 212, 215). For up-to-date country-specific information on profiling methods see IAB (2005).

CONCLUSIONS: A FRAMEWORK FOR THE MANAGEMENT OF CHANGE

9

From our overview of (active) labour market policies around the world it is possible to identify some general principles, despite the great diversity of situations across the globe and the scarcity of information, especially for developing countries, both of which make it all but impossible to arrive at a concise typology. A first observation is that ALMPs have been in use for some time in all regions of the world, and that developing countries in general prefer active programmes related to work and training over passive, purely income-related measures such as unemployment benefit systems. In the developed world, however, despite all the discussions on the preference for active rather than passive labour market policies, the latter predominate by about 2:1. This applies to LMP programmes viewed overall. However, in specific areas, such as worker retrenchment, despite the lack of systematic information, it seems that passive, income-related programmes, for example severance pay, are preferred to active measures in the developing world too.

This said, we acknowledge a wide variation across the globe in the dimensions of labour market problems. This in turn affects the choice of policies to be applied. The transition of young people from school to work requires different solutions from the reintegration of older job losers into the labour market. Likewise, the jobless single mother needs a different combination of income and work from an unemployed young person without children. The informal worker might need only an in-work benefit to obtain a decent income, while the drought-stricken subsistence farmer might need to participate in a well-organized public works irrigation project that (re)creates the conditions for sustainable self-employed farming. Some people need only access to micro-credits to set up their own business activity, whereas others first need basic training. Large-scale retrenchment programmes, which have emerged in all the countries that embarked on the transition from a planned to a market economy, usually need a whole series of labour market policy tools from severance pay to retraining and temporary public work schemes, as well as adequate labour market services to implement such programmes.

Very schematically, these differences have to do with the sheer extent of the economic and social problems related to unemployment, underemployment and poverty. If the supply-side pressures are such that there is no possible quantitative match in terms of demand, any bridging between supply and demand, which is the primary function of LMPs, seems at first sight to be senseless.

However, adopting a broader definition, as we did in this study, gives some support for the use of ALMPs – even in the face of large over-supply – because of the combined effect of their macroeconomic function (multipliers) and the intrinsic value of income derived from productive work for society on the condition that, in such circumstances, the demand-side elements (e.g. public works, entrepreneurial support) are dominant or that at least supply-side and demand-side measures are integrated in programmes. In addition, it has to be considered that ALMPs in developing countries often take on a different function from that performed in developed countries: in developing countries they are often the only means of ensuring income subsistence in the case of unemployment, while in all developed OECD countries unemployment benefit systems usually exist and ALMPs come on top of these, usually serving the longer-term unemployed and/or activating these passive measures. This study has shown that ALMP measures that now seem less important in some developed OECD countries, such as public works and demand-side measures in general, can be very successful in developing countries.

The solutions adopted will also depend on the financial capacity of countries and the opportunity costs of ALMP spending: if money available for employment purposes can be spent more effectively than through ALMPs, these opportunities should of course be used. However, in many countries these alternatives are either non-existent or yield less direct employment results. There might be cheaper alternatives (such as preferring passive over active measures), but they are usually less efficient in terms of combating the economic and social problems linked to unemployment and underemployment.

This leads on to a related problem: in some countries (e.g. in Latin America) larger-scale ALMP programmes are de facto increasingly transformed into income-replacement programmes without work or training content, because of a low capacity to **organize** ALMPs effectively. Paying a stipend to those in need also poses an organizational challenge, but is usually much easier than organizing meaningful work or training for those out of work. Basic questions arise here on the most appropriate framework for organizing the work content of social welfare: in general this has to be done on a local basis and thus within decentralized administrative structures. It can be done by both public and private (both for profit and non-profit) organizations. But organization is required and in matters of (in our case "labour market") governance, the recent report of the World Commission on the Social Dimension of Globalization puts forward a claim for "an effective State ... that provides public goods and social protection [and] raises the capabilities of people" (WCSDG, 2004, p. xii).

The presence of any formal framework, such as a strong ministry and/or labour administration with a good local outreach, certainly influences favourably any effort to set up or expand ALMPs. But while the absence of organization is clearly a major barrier for successful implementation of ALMPs, the presence of strong labour market administration alone does not guarantee its success. Some European countries that have a comprehensive and strong labour administration face problems in coping with a continuous flow of unemployed people. The crucial questions are: What is the most appropriate form of labour market administration today? Should it be organized publicly or privately? Should it be decentralized or centralized? Should it serve only the needy or all labour market participants? What are the respective roles of active and passive policies? What does an adequate distribution of responsibilities look like? There are partial answers to these questions: public/private interaction with clearly defined roles; decentralized frameworks with a basic function of monitoring, feedback and control for central units; a focus on the harder-to-place and preference for active measures. However, each national labour market, and its administrative framework, is highly specific, and careful interrogation of these general principles is necessary in order to make particular recommendations.

On the other hand, there are also generally valid recommendations that deal with certain principles of ALMPs. For example, in order to make ALMPs work **they should evolve towards a more permanent policy instrument for the management of change** rather than being a quick-fix solution for emergencies. However, the permanency of the instruments should not lead to the permanency of people placed in them. In the past, observers have noted that while programmes often change, participants can remain in them for a long time. Rather than temporary institutions taking care permanently of the same individuals with labour market problems, one needs permanent but adaptable institutions that temporarily take care of individuals with labour market problems and integrate them effectively into the labour market. The institutionalization of ALMPs would also allow them to function as an "automatic stabilizer" in the economy (Quiggin, 2001). The **bridge** rather than the **trap** function has to be dominant in modern ALMPs. We see LMPs in general and ALMPs in particular as a labour market governance instrument of great relevance to countries that aim to introduce more coherence and security into their labour markets without necessarily introducing new rigidities. This principle appears to be valid for all regions in the world, as they all are and will be affected by change in the wake of globalization. However, the dimensions of the problems, and thus the necessary solutions, can differ radically from one region to another. For example, the mere quantitative gap between labour supply and demand, even leaving aside the informal labour market, is enormous in developing countries. There the main problem is youth entry into the labour market; worker redundancy is significant, but secondary. In contrast, OECD countries increasingly have to face new labour market and social security challenges resulting not only from demographic changes, such as workforce ageing, but also from women's growing participation in the labour market. The gap between labour supply and demand seems to be much greater in transition countries than in advanced industrialized countries, where quantitative gaps exist, but where the quality (structural) dimension (by skills/location) is equally important. In both regions, the entry problems of first-time jobseekers and exit problems of those losing jobs are more balanced than in developing countries.

The relationship between ALMPs and the informal economy requires special attention. ALMPs such as training could be used to enhance the productivity of informal workers, while public works can build infrastructure, providing a first step towards formalization. Other policies such as **in-work**

benefits could act as an incentive to formalize jobs. In addition, self-employment measures that suit only a small group of the unemployed in OECD and transition countries are in many developing countries large in scope and successful. The relationship between the informal economy – consisting of a large number of informal entrepreneurs – and such measures of support as might help the emergence of a more formal segment of entrepreneurial activity should be borne in mind when designing self-employment promotion programmes.

The list of variation of needs is long, and while **there is no single solution for every individual, there is also no "one-size-fits-all" solution either**. There is a need to balance supply- and demand-side measures and to analyse carefully local employment problems and the basic characteristics of participants, as well as the delivery system in the country or locality. All these characteristics have to be matched: employment problems to labour market policy measures, individual characteristics to labour market programmes, and programmes to individuals.

Best-practice examples should be used, but there is no guarantee that policies that are successful in one country will also work in another country or region; they have to be carefully adapted to the local situation. Therefore each national ALMP framework has to start with a thorough problem assessment.

More fundamental problems are linked to the absence of funding, and to weak organizational and administrative capacities, which for example very often turn impressive work-based programmes into mere income-replacement schemes, even in situations where work (but not employment) abounds.

Differences in the use of policy instruments stem partly from differences in the organization of the delivery institutions. While all countries are currently trying to set up or enhance labour market institutions such as employment services, unemployment insurance systems, labour market information systems and ALMPs, these institutions are as yet rather ineffective in delivering job matching, benefit administration or ALMP implementation. While evidence points to the **advantages of decentralization**, there is also a need for central coordination and monitoring, especially in situations of weak local delivery institutions and/or when there is a danger of "nepotism" and corruption. However, there is a need for a strong local focus when it comes to programme implementation in order to be able to adapt policies better to the specific local labour market situations and needs.

There is also a need for policy integration. For example, in order to run activation programmes (transfer payments made conditional on participation in work or training programmes) efficiently, public employment services should integrate benefit payments and placement activities, or at least have available the information on claimants and their work history. A way to tackle the direct integration of policies, which can run into problems to do with frameworks of organization, interest and power (e.g. when ministries of labour and of welfare are separated) is the cooperation in the organization of so-called one-stop shops that provide a single service interface for the individual, while the back offices can remain separated.

Integration is required not only for delivery institutions but also at the programme level. It has been found that multi-purpose programmes (such as working while being trained) yield some advantages over single-purpose programmes. Intelligent programme integration should therefore be a task for programme designers of ALMPs.

Scarcity of funding is a major obstacle, especially in developing countries. Here new ways of funding should be envisaged. One possible way could be **to make donors embrace the goals of ALMPs and align their funds for this purpose**. Integrating ALMPs into PRSPs (Poverty Reduction Strategy Papers: the growth and poverty-alleviation strategies driven by the World Bank and IMF but owned by countries) would be a step towards channelling funds to ALMPs.

Finally, the design and implementation of ALMPs is both an area of **active coordination and policy integration** between ministries concerned (e.g. employment, labour, social affairs, finance, economy, agriculture) and an important field for **social partner involvement**. Although the unemployed, the underemployed, the poor and the working poor of the informal economy are usually not the main constituents of business and labour, they are potential formal employees. In so far as they are represented by other organs of civil society, the main social partners in industry should seek cooperation with civil society in order to gain knowledge of these workers' needs, thereby helping to solve their labour market problems.

In conclusion, then, active labour market policies, together with passive, income protection policies such as unemployment benefits, are an important tool for labour market governance in open economies. They are supported by the social partners (see Rychly and Vylitova, 2005). They play a strong role as a security element in labour markets that have been organized along flexicurity principles and are thus indispensable elements of labour market security in the globalizing world. Despite shortcomings revealed by labour market policy evaluation – which prompt the call for policy action and even an evaluation "culture", as called for by the European Commission) – they are the most direct lever of action on the labour market and as such a much-needed instrument in the toolkit of employment policy.

While this applies generally, the concrete design and policy mix (between active and passive, between supply- and demand-side policies) will differ from country to country. In some low-income developing countries, the basic ingredients for labour market security are either not developed at all,[1] or are too poorly developed to trigger any protection, and hence the term indicates only the gaps to be filled by policy action, which however is constrained by lack of financing and lack of effective institutions. In other countries, elements of the system exist and can be enhanced. But there is no escape: those who care about workers' welfare and decent work, and believe that there is no trade-off between social and economic goals, must seek credible security solutions that necessarily include ALMPs.

95

Note

[1] The necessary elements are employment protection, social protection and social dialogue, the last of the three holding the first two in balance to achieve flexicurity.

BIBLIOGRAPHY

Abate-Franjul, F. 2006. "The continent's poor: A new niche for traditional banks?", in *Microenterprise Development Review*, Vol. 9, No. 2 (Washington, DC, Inter-American Development Bank).

Agell, J. 1999. "On the benefits from rigid labour markets: Norms, market failures and social insurance", in *Economic Journal*, Vol. 109, No. 453, p. 143 ff.

Asian Productivity Organization. 2002a. *Education and training of rural youth*, Report of the APO Seminar on Education and Training of Rural Youth, Japan, 15-22 Aug. 2001 (Tokyo).

—. 2002b. *Education and training of rural women in Asia and the Pacific*, Report of the APO Seminar on Education and Training of Rural Women, Tokyo, 23 Feb.-2 Mar. 2000 (Tokyo).

Auer, P. 2000. *Employment revival in Europe* (Geneva, ILO).

—. 2001. *Labour market policies for socially responsible workforce adjustment*, Employment Paper 2001/14 (Geneva, ILO).

—. 2007. "In search of optimal labour market institutions", in H. Jorgensen and P.K. Madsen (eds): *Flexicurity and beyond: Finding a new agenda for the European social model* (Copenhagen, DJOF Publishing), pp. 67-98.

—; Cazes, S. (eds). 2003. *Employment stability in an age of flexibility: Evidence from industrialized countries* (Geneva, ILO).

—; Berg, J.; Coulibaly, I. 2004. *Is a more stable workforce good for the economy? Insights into the tenure-productivity-employment relationship*, Employment Strategy Paper (Geneva, ILO).

—; Kruppe, T. 1996. "Monitoring of labour market policy in EU Member States", in G. Schmid et al. (eds): *International handbook of labour market policy and evaluation* (Cheltenham, Edward Elgar), pp. 899-920.

Beleva, I.; Tzanov, V.; Tisheva, G. 2006. "Bulgaria", in S. Cazes and A. Nesporova (eds): *Flexicurity: A relevant approach in Central and Eastern Europe* (Geneva, ILO), pp. 57-92.

Betcherman, G.; Dar, A.; Luinstra, A.; Ogawa, M. 2001. "Active labour market policies: Issues for East Asia", in G. Betcherman and R. Islam (eds): *East Asian labour markets and the economic crisis: Impacts, responses and lessons* (Washington, DC, International Bank for Reconstruction and Development/The World Bank), pp. 295-344.

—; Islam, R. (eds). 2001. *East Asian labour markets and the economic crisis: Impacts, responses and lessons* (Washington, DC, International Bank for Reconstruction and Development/The World Bank).

—; Olivas, K.; Dar, A. 2004. *Impacts of active labour market programs: New evidence from evaluations with particular attention to developing and transition countries*, Social Protection Discussion Paper Series 402 (Washington, DC, The World Bank).

Björklund, A.; Regnér, H. 1996. "Experimental evaluation of European labour market policy", in G. Schmid et al. (eds): *International handbook of labour market policy and evaluation* (Cheltenham, Edward Elgar), pp. 89-114.

Bundesanstalt für Arbeit. 1999. *Jahreszahlen 1998* (Annual Data 1998), online source: http://www.pub.arbeitsmat.de/hst/services/anba/jg_1999/jz98/r519.

—. 2003. *Arbeitsbeschaffungsmaßnahmen* (Job creation programmes), Referat IIIb3, online source: http://www.pub.arbeitsamt.de/hst/services/statistik/ detail/a.html.

Cazes, S.; Nesporova, A. 2003. *Labour markets in transition: Balancing flexibility and security in Central and Eastern Europe* (Geneva, ILO).

— (eds.). 2007. *Flexicurity: A relevant approach in Central and Eastern Europe* (Geneva, ILO).

Chimerine, L.; Black, T.; Coffey, L. 1999. *Unemployment insurance as an automatic stabilizer: Evidence of effectiveness over three decades*, Occasional Paper 99-8 (Washington, DC, US Department of Labor).

Dar, A.; Tzannatos, T. 1999. *Active labor market programs: A review of the evidence from evaluations*, Social Protection Discussion Paper Series 9901 (Washington, DC, World Bank).

—; Amirkhalkhali, S. 2003. "On the impact of trade openness on growth: Further evidence from OECD countries", in *Applied Economics*, Vol. 35, No. 16.

De Ferranti, D.; Perry, G.E.; Gill, I.S.; Servén, L. 2000. *Securing our future in a global economy*, World Bank Latin American and Caribbean Studies (Washington, DC, International Bank for Reconstruction and Development/The World Bank).

Devereux, S. 2002. *From workfare to fair work: The contribution of public works and other labour-based infrastructure programmes to poverty alleviation*, Issues in Employment and Poverty Discussion Paper No. 5 (Geneva, ILO).

Direction de l'animation de la recherche, des études et des statistiques (DARES). 1996. *40 ans de politique de l'emploi* (Paris, La Documentation Française).

Erhel, C.; Gautié, J.; Gazier, B.; Morel, S. 1996. "Job opportunities for the hard-to-place", in G. Schmid et al. (eds): *International handbook of labour market policy and evaluation* (Cheltenham, Edward Elgar), pp. 277-307.

Esser, D.; Ozoux, P.; Rogovsky, N. 2003. *Socially sensitive enterprise restructuring*, Tripartite Training Module (Geneva, ILO).

European Commission 2006. *Employment in Europe 2006* (Brussels), esp. chapter on "Effective European active labour market policies", http://ec. europa. eu/employment_social/employment_analysis/eie/eie2006_chap3_en.pdf.

—. 2007. Communication from the Commission to the Council, the European Parliament, the European Economic and Social Committee and the Committee of the Regions, "Towards common principles of flexicurity: More and better jobs through flexibility and security" (Brussels).

European Council. 2005. Council Decision of 12 July 2005 on guidelines for the employment policies of Member States (2005/600/EC), *Official Journal of the European Union*, http://eur-lex.europa.eu/LexUriServ/site /en/oj/2005/l_205/l_20520050806en 00210027.pdf.

Eurostat. 2007. "Labour force survey", New Cronos database, http://epp.eurostat.cec.eu.int/.

Fay, R.G. 1996. *Enhancing the effectiveness of active labour market policies: Evidence from programme evaluation in OECD countries*, Labour Market and Social Policy Occasional Papers, No. 18 (Paris, OECD).

Fortuny, M.; Nesporova, A.; Popova, N. 2003. *Employment promotion policies for older workers in the EU accession countries, the Russian Federation and Ukraine* (Geneva, ILO).

Frey, M. 2007. "Legal and institutional environment of the Hungarian labour market", in Fazekas, K. et al. (eds.): *The Hungarian labour market. Review and analysis 2007* (Budapest, Institute of Economics, HAS Hungarian Employment Foundation), pp. 129-159.

Galhardi, R. 2002. *Financing training: Innovative approaches in Latin America*, ILO InFocus Programme on Skills, Knowledge and Employability, Skills Working Paper No. 12, prepared for the International IVETA 2002 Conference, Mauritius, 20-24 July 2002.

Gilbert, N.; Van Voorhis, A. (eds). 2001. *A comparative appraisal of work-oriented policies: Activating the unemployed*, International Social Security Series, Vol. 3 (New Brunswick/London, Transaction Publishers).

Gruber, J. 1997. "The consumption smoothing benefits of unemployment insurance", in *American Economic Review*, Vol. 87, No.1, pp. 192-205.

Handoussa, H.; Tzannatos, Z. 2002. *Employment creation and social protection in the Middle East and North Africa* (Cairo, The American University in Cairo Press).

Hansen, G.B. 2001. *A guide to worker displacement* (Geneva, ILO InFocus Programme on Skills, Knowledge and Employability).

Institut für Arbeits- und Berufsforschung (IAB). 2005. *Profiling for better services* (H. Rudolph; R. Konle-Seidl), Report on the European Profiling Seminar, Nuremberg, 12-14 Jan., supported by EU Commission (DG Empl) VP/2004/007.

International Labour Office (ILO). 2000. *Employing youth: Promoting employment-intensive growth, Report for the interregional symposium on strategies to combat youth unemployment and marginalization*, Geneva, 13-14 Dec. 1999 (Geneva).

—. 2001. 2001 *Labour overview: Latin America and the Caribbean* (Lima).

—. 2002a. *Micro-finance in industrialized countries: Helping the unemployed to start business* (Geneva, ILO, Employment Sector, Social Finance Programme).

—. 2002b. *Modernization in vocational education and training in the Latin American and the Caribbean Region*, Skills Working Paper No. 4 (Geneva, ILO, InFocus Programme on Skills, Knowledge and Employability).

—. 2003a. *Review of the core elements of the Global Employment Agenda*, Governing Body, Committee on Employment and Social Policy, GB.286/ESP/1(Rev.), 286th Session, Geneva, 2003.

—. 2003b. *Time for equality at work*, Global Report under the Follow-up to the ILO Declaration on Fundamental Principles and Rights at Work, Report I, International Labour Conference, 91st Session, Geneva, 2003.

—. 2003c. *Working out of poverty*, Report of the Director-General, Report I(A), International Labour Conference, 91st Session, Geneva, 2003.

—. 2004. *Economic security for a better world* (Geneva).

—. 2007. "Progress evaluation of the Social Trust Pilot project", 300th session of the Governing Body, Geneva, Nov., GB 300/ESP/5.

Kanyenze, G.; Mhone, G.C.Z.; Sparreboom, T. 2000. *Strategies to combat youth unemployment and marginalisation in anglophone Africa*, Discussion Paper No. 14 (Harare, ILO, Southern Africa Multidisciplinary Advisory Team [ILO/SAMAT]).

Kluve J. et al. 2005. *Study on the effectiveness of ALMPs*, Research project for the European Commission, DG Employment, Social Affairs and Equal Opportunities, final report, http://ec.europa.eu/employment_social/incentive _measures/studies/effect_imp_almp_fin_rep_en.pdf.

Kwiatkowski, E.; Socha, M.; Sztanderska, U. 2001. *Labour market flexibility and employment security: Poland*, Employment Paper 2001/28 (Geneva, ILO).

Levitsky, J.; Hojmark Mikkelsen, L. 2001. *Micro- and small enterprises in Latin America: Experience of business development services* (Washington, DC, Inter-American Development Bank).

Lim, L.L.; Sziraczki, G. (eds). 1995. *Employment challenges and policy responses: Chinese and international perspectives* (ILO Beijing Area Office).

Llisterri, J. 2006. "Credit guarantee systems in Latin America: Taking stock", in *Micro-enterprise Development Review*, Vol. 9, No. 2 (Washington, DC, Inter-American Development Bank).

Lyby, E. 2001. *From destruction to reconstruction: The Uganda experience 1981-1997 using employment-intensive technology* (Geneva, ILO, Recovery and Reconstruction Department).

Márquez, G. 1999. *Unemployment insurance and emergency employment programs in Latin America and the Caribbean: An overview*, paper for the Conference on Social Protection and Poverty (Washington, DC, Inter-American Development Bank).

—. 2002. *Training the workforce in Latin America: What needs to be done?*, Labor Markets Policy Briefs Series (Washington, DC, Inter-American Development Bank).

Marshall, A. 1997. *State labour market intervention in Argentina, Chile and Uruguay: Common model, different versions* (Geneva, ILO, Employment and Training Department).

—. 2004. *Labour market policies and regulations in Argentina, Brazil and Mexico: Programmes and impacts*, Employment Strategy Papers (Geneva, ILO, Employment Strategy Department).

Martin, J.P. 1998. *What works among active labour market policies: Evidence from OECD countries' experiences*, Labour Market and Social Policy Occasional Paper No. 35 (Paris, OECD).

—. 2000. "What works among active labour market policies: Evidence from OECD countries' experiences", in *Economic Studies*, Vol. 30 (Paris, OECD), pp. 106-107.

—; Grubb, D. 2001. "What works and for whom: A review of OECD countries' experiences with active labour market policies", in *Swedish Economic Policy Review*, Vol. 8, pp. 9-56.

Mazza, J. 2000. *Unemployment insurance: case studies and lessons for Latin America and the Carribean*, Working Paper Series No. 411 (Washington, DC, Inter-American Development Bank).

—. 2003. "Labour intermediation services: Lessons for Latin America and the Caribbean", in *CEPAL Review*, Vol. 80, No. 2, pp. 159-175.

Meager, N.; Evans, C. 1998. *The evaluation of active labour market measures for the long-term unemployed*, Employment and Training Paper No.16 (Geneva, ILO).

Ministério do Trabalho e Emprego. 2007. *Programa de Geração de Emprego, Trabalho e Renda (PROGER)*, http://www.mte.gov.br/proger/default.asp.

Moura Castro, C.; de Schaack, K.; Tippelt, R. (eds). 2000. *Vocational training at the turn of the century*, Beiträge zur Bildungsplanung und Bildungsökonomie (Frankfurt am Main, Europäischer Verlag der Wissenschaft).

Nesporova, A. 1999. *Employment and labour market policies in transition economies* (Geneva, ILO, Employment and Training Department, Employment and Labour Market Policies Branch).

O'Leary, C.; Kolodziejczyk, P.; Lázár, G. 1998. "The net impact of active labour programmes in Hungary and Poland", in *International Labour Review*, Vol. 137, No. 3, pp. 321-346.

—; Nesporova, A.; Samorodov, A. 2001. *Manual on evaluation of labour market policies in transition economies* (Geneva, ILO).

Organisation for Economic Co-operation and Development (OECD). 1993. "Active labour market policies: Assessing the macroeconomic and microeconomic effects", in *OECD Employment Outlook* (Paris), pp. 39-80.

—. 1996. *OECD jobs strategy: Enhancing the effectiveness of active labour market policies* (Paris).

—. 2000. *Labour market policies and the public employment service*, Prague Conference, July 2000.

—. 2001a. *Knowledge, work organisation and economic growth*, Labour Market and Social Policy Occasional Papers, No. 50, DEELSA/ELSA/WD 20013 (Paris).

—. 2001b. *Employment Outlook 2001* (Paris).

—. 2002. *Employment Outlook 2002* (Paris).

—. 2003a. "Making work pay, making work possible", in *Employment Outlook 2003* (Paris), pp. 113-170.

—. 2003b. "Upgrading workers' skills and competencies", in *Employment Outlook 2003* (Paris), pp. 237-296.

—. 2004. *Employment Outlook 2004* (Paris).

—. 2005a. "Public employment services: Managing performance", in *Employment Outlook 2005* (Paris), pp. 209-233.

—. 2005b. "Increasing financial incentives to work: The role of in-work-benefits", in *Employment Outlook 2005* (Paris), pp. 125-171.

—. 2005c. "Labour market programmes and activation strategies: Evaluating the impacts", in *Employment Outlook 2005* (Paris), pp. 137 ff.

—. 2007a. *Employment Outlook 2007* (Paris).

—. 2007b. Statistics Portal (Paris), http://www.oecd.org/statsportal/0,3352, en_2825_293564_1_1_1_1_1,00.html.

—. 2007c. "Activating the unemployed: What countries do", in *Employment Outlook 2007* (Paris), pp. 207-242.

Orszag, P. 2001. *Unemployment insurance as economic stimulus*, Policy Brief (Washington, DC, Center on Budget and Policy Priorities).

Quiggin, J. 2001. "Active labour market policy and macroeconomic stabilisation", in *The Drawing Board – Australian Review of Public Affairs* (Sydney, University of Sydney).

Reinecke, G.; White, S. 2004. *Policies for small enterprises: Creating the right environment for good jobs* (Geneva, ILO).

Rogovsky, N. 2000. *Corporate community involvement programmes: Partnerships for jobs and development*, Working Paper No. DP/116/2000 (Geneva, International Institute for Labour Studies, Business and Society Programme).

Rogovsky, N. (ed.). 2005. *Restructuring for corporate success: A socially sensitive approach* (Geneva, ILO).

Rychly, L.; Vylitova, M. 2005. *National social dialogue on employment policies in Europe* (Geneva, ILO, Social Dialogue, Labour Law and Labour Administration Department).

Schmid, G. 1996. "New public management of further training", in G. Schmid et al. (eds): *International handbook of labour market policy and evaluation* (Cheltenham, Edward Elgar), pp. 747-790.

—; O'Reilly, J.; Schömann, K. 1996. "Theory and methodology of labour market policy and evaluation: An introduction", in G. Schmid et al. (eds): *International handbook of labour market policy and evaluation* (Cheltenham, Edward Elgar), pp. 1-33.

—; Gazier, B. (eds). 2002. *The dynamics of full employment: Social integration through transitional labour markets* (Cheltenham, Edward Elgar).

—; Reissert, B.; Bruche, G. 1992. *Unemployment insurance and active labor market policy. An international comparison of financing systems* (Detroit, Wayne State University Press).

Schömann, K.; O'Connell, P. (eds). 2002. *Education, training and employment dynamics: Transitional labour markets in the European Union* (Cheltenham, Edward Elgar).

Schulz, G.; Klemmer, B. 1998. *Public employment services in English-speaking Africa: Proposals for re-organization* (Harare, ILO, African Regional Labour Administration Centre (ARLAC), Employment Service Project).

Secretaría de medio ambiente y recursos naturals (SEMARNAT). 2007. *Programa de empleo temporal* (Mexico), http://www.semarnat.gob.mx /queessemarnat/programas/Pages/ pet.aspx.

Sen, A. 1989. "Development or capability expansion", in *Journal of Development Planning*, Vol. 19 (New York), pp. 41-58.

Spitznagel, E. 1975. "Arbeitsmarktpolitische Massnahmen: Entlastungswirkungen und Kostenvergleiche" (Labour market policy measures: Employment effects and cost comparisons), in *MittAB (Mitteilungen aus der Arbeitsmarkt und Berufsforschung)*, 1/1975.

Tchetvernina, T.; Moscovskaya, A.; Soboleva, I.; Stepantchikova, N. 2001. *Labour market flexibility and employment security: Russian Federation*, Employment Paper 2001/31 (Geneva, ILO).

Thuy, P.; Hansen, E.; Price, D. 2001. *The public employment service in a changing labour market* (Geneva, ILO).

Večernik, J. 2001. *Labour market flexibility and employment security: Czech Republic*, Employment Paper Series 2001/27 (Geneva, ILO).

World Commission on the Social Dimension of Globalization (WCSDG). 2004. *A fair globalization: Creating opportunities for all* (Geneva, ILO).

Wolter, S. 1998. "The cost of job-insecurity: Results from Switzerland", in *International Journal of Manpower*, Vol. 19, No. 6, pp. 396-409.

LIST OF ABBREVIATIONS

ALMP   active labour market policy

CETA   Comprehensive Employment and Training Act (US)

EES   European Employment Strategy of the European Commission
EITC   Earned Income Tax Credit (US)

GEA   Global Employment Agenda

LMP   labour market policy
LMT   labour market training

NES   national employment service
NGO   non-governmental organization

PES   public employment services
PLMP   passive labour market policy
PRSP   Poverty Reduction Strategy Paper (World Bank/IMF)
PW   public works

SE   subsidized employment
SMEs   small and medium-sized enterprises

WFTC   Working Families' Tax Credit (UK)

YEN   Youth Employment Network